TEC COMMUNICATION CONSTRUCTION WORK

Brian Rowe, BA,
Lecturer,
Haywards Heath College

and

R. H. Jinks, MA, Dip Ed,
Principal Lecturer,
Brighton Technical College

HODDER AND STOUGHTON
LONDON SYDNEY AUCKLAND TORONTO

British Library Cataloguing in Publication Data
Rowe, Brian
 TEC communications for construction work.
 1. English language – Technical English
 2. Building – Language
 I. Title   II. Jinks, R H
 428'.002'4624   PE1116.B/

ISBN 0 340 23044 4

Copyright © 1980 by Brian Rowe and R. Jinks
All rights reserved. No part of this publication may be reproduced or transmitted in any form or by any means, electronic or mechanical, including photocopy, recording, or any information storage and retrieval system, without permission in writing from the publisher.

Phototypeset in V.I.P. Century Schoolbook by
Western Printing Services Ltd, Bristol

Printed in Great Britain for
Hodder and Stoughton Educational,
a division of Hodder and Stoughton Ltd,
Mill Road, Dunton Green, Sevenoaks, Kent,
by Biddles Ltd, Guildford, Surrey

Contents

Introduction		v
Unit 1	Comprehension; Discussion; Drafting a notice; Letter writing; Discussion work	1
Unit 2	Comprehension; Critical Work; Elementary research; Organization of material	7
Unit 3	Comprehension; Discussion	11
Unit 4	Note-taking; Comprehension and critical work: Work on statistics; Narrative report	15
Unit 5	Multiple Choice Comprehension; Research and organization of material; Research; Discussion	21
Unit 6	Comprehension and summarizing; Technical writing: definitions; Vocabulary	27
Unit 7	Comprehension with research; Organization of material; Punctuation and spelling	31
Unit 8	Comprehension; Critical work; Discussion; Drafting a notice	35
Unit 9	Technical comprehension and technical work; Technical material; Technical vocabulary	39
Unit 10	Comprehension; Letter writing	43
Unit 11	Comprehension; Research; Letter writing; Vocabulary	48
Unit 12	Note-taking; Technical vocabulary and description	52
Unit 13	Discussion; personal writing; Verse study; Technical description; Use of hyphens	55
Unit 14	Discussion; Practical work; Research and letter writing	60
Unit 15	Comprehension; Practical work; Lecturette; Writing an advertisement; Vocabulary	64
Unit 16	The Summary (1); General; Writing	69
Unit 17	The Summary (2); General; Vocabulary	73
Unit 18	Summary; Writing; Discussion; Vocabulary; Punctuation	78
Unit 19	Comprehension; Summary	82
Unit 20	Comprehension; Summary; Discussion; Writing; Essay writing; Letter writing	86
Unit 21	Comprehension; Writing; Vocabulary	90
Unit 22	Comprehension; Punctuation	95
Unit 23	Technical diagrams; Punctuation (revision); Letter writing and form filling	99

Unit 24	Comprehension; Punctuation	102
Unit 25	Comprehension; Punctuation; Vocabulary	107
Unit 26	Minute writing; Discussion	111
Unit 27	Multiple Choice Comprehension; Summary; Writing; Oral	116
Unit 28	Comprehension; Note-making	121
Unit 29	Oral work; Summary	125
Unit 30	Multiple Choice Comprehension; Notes and research; Notes and report; Writing	130
Unit 31	Suggested Projects	136
Acknowledgments		137

Introduction

The aim of this book is to provide sufficient work in English and Communications for students on a TEC Construction course. It has been designed after a careful study of the requirements of a wide variety of TEC College submissions which have been accepted, yet most of the material will also be immediately relevant to students on other construction courses. While many of the passages and exercises relate directly to technical material, others are less specific and lead outwards towards the General Studies areas of the courses.

The chapters are planned to help the student to develop his understanding and control of language progressively; however, each chapter is planned as a self-standing unit to enable lecturers who prefer to plan and organize the development of their own courses to make use of specific chapters or exercises without necessarily using the book as a base for their course.

The majority of the exercises are designed to meet the practical vocational interests of the students, but a few sections and exercises have been included which are intended to provide at least an introduction to the more formal elements in language study such as still occur in traditional English language examinations. Most TEC submissions, rightly in our view, largely exclude such elements as the formal essay and summary; it is nevertheless likely that a number of TEC students will at a later date wish to apply for entry to Higher Education for which a qualification in English language is frequently demanded. In view of this, some of the work included provides the student with an insight into and practice in the type of exercises they will then need to grapple with.

Unit 1

Comprehension (including discussion material)

Arthur Haggerson is fifteen and has just left school. The following passage describes the first few hours of his first day at work. He has no father, and the job has been found for him by his Uncle George. After reading the passage, answer the questions below.

The site was a fifty yard strip of waste land gently descending to the river a mile or so away. There was a little burn running through it. The trench ran parallel. There was a concrete mixer with a couple of feeder bunkers, the big digger, stacks of concrete piping maybe six feet in diameter, a compressor, and a shed. Apart from the hum of voices in the shed it was the picture of a quiet Sabbath morning, lacking only the bells.

I put my bike against the shed and stuck my nose through the door – and that's all there was room for. The place was jammed tight. Some characters sitting around the sides were getting their beauty sleep out. Those conscious were sitting or standing around a table at the head of which was a character with a face like a frog writing bets on a sheet of paper and checking up on a pile of change.

Nobody noticed me.

'Where's the foreman?' I asked.

Character near the door stitching a patch on a pair of overalls shouted back, 'What you want?'

'Ah'm lookin' for the foreman.'

'Pipe down everybody,' said the bookie. The funny thing was that they did pipe down. 'Now what's it all about?'

'Ah'm lookin' for the foreman.'

'Now that's a change!' he remarked, 'Soon knock that out of ye. You the gaffer's nevvy?' I nodded.

'You don't sound it. Didn't he tell ye to report to the assistant bumper-up?'

'All he said was to be here at seven.'

'Kiddar, you certainly started well – it's ten past seven.'

'I got a puncture.'

'Here – wait a minute,' he said. 'Stand on that step – that's right, up a bit.' He put his thumbs in his waistcoat and stood up to get a better view. Everybody was looking. 'Why, man, it must be all of twenty years since Ah saw a pair of pure-bred moleskins,' he said. 'Just look at them.'

'Brightness as well as whiteness,' said the character with the needle.

'Where's his gun belt?'

'Well, well,' said the bookie. 'First thing you can do is drag them trousers through the burn an' make yourself a man.'

'You go an' stuff yourself,' I said. Feller with a long nose gave a low whistle. Didn't take any notice – I was starting as I intended to finish. No bookie's runner was going to rub my nose in the dirt.

'Hey,' he said. 'It's a comedian.'

'Listen,' I told him. 'These trousers'll take off but you've got to wear that face.'

He didn't like it but put on a good laugh. 'Listen to that,' he told the others. 'Like his uncle he's a good talker . . . now just wait a minute son till Ah get the job organized and then we'll have a bit talk.'

He told the gang off and cleared the place in next to no time. In a couple of minutes I could hear the compressor going and the lorries rolling. Could see what he meant by bumper-up.

After they'd gone he counted up the suckers' money, and made out some timesheets. Getting bored I sat down. He finished his work and sat tapping his pencil, buff-end, on the table. At the same time he was grinning.

At last he said: 'Think a bit about yourself, son, don't ye?'

'Don't like havin' the soft picked outa me.'

'What's your first name?'

'Arthur.'

'Well, Arthur; you better get to know the strength of the job. Don't lean on Uncle George too much. In fact, don't lean on anybody. Not that ye'll get much chance to lean on Uncle George because most of the time he isn't around. He's a very busy man, is Uncle George, an' depends upon me. My name's Sprogget – Mr. Sprogget to you.'

'Okay, Mr. Sprogget.'

'That's a good lad. Now hop over to the mixer an' tell George Flack to show you a shovel.'

'What's that?'

'George Flack. And son. . . ?'

'Yes?'

'Better not mention my face again.'

I didn't say anything. Just gave him a dead-pan look and

walked out. Strike like a snake and never give, that's the technique. But underneath I was as nervous as a kitten. I didn't like the look of the assistant bumper-up. He was the original snake.

Flack was the character with the big nose. The lorries were dumping loads of pebbles and he was shovelling the stuff through a sheet screen. My job was to load the stuff on to an endless conveyor that fed the bunkers feeding the mixer. Old Flack gave me a shovel and showed me where to put it, then stood watching my paces with a genial sneer which set his face askew. In the end he took the shovel and showed me how to hold it, and I thanked him.

He walked back to the other side of the screen and scratched his nose. 'You got a nerve,' he said. Then his face crumpled into a grin. 'Yes – he's got a face all right – can't do anything else but wear it.' He kept shovelling hard and every ten minutes or so let off a burst of machine-gun laughter. But he didn't say anything else until about nine o'clock maybe. 'Better go and mash some tea, kiddar,' he told me. 'Kettle's in the shed.'

I laid the shovel down gently but it was no good. My right hand had been operated on. There were aches all over the territory. 'You'll learn to let the shovel do the work,' he said. 'And you go canny with Sprogget; he's a naughty character.'

I was an inch short of six feet and getting on for twelve stone. 'Reckon Ah can look after myself,' I told him.

'Well, it gets monotonous,' he said. That's all. And picked up his shovel again. I made the tea and the gang gathered round. That's when Uncle George arrived. He wandered over. He looked at everybody but me, then said to Sprogget: 'How's she goin'?'

'Fine, George,' said the bookie. 'New man came late, that's all.'

He just grunted. 'Let's have a look at the pegs,' he said; and they wandered off together. I reckon that's when I knew what he was. He didn't look at me or say a word, and it all added up to the fact that I was dirt or something of that order. You can imagine me standing there with the big teapot in my hand, jaw on my chin, eyes mad. Some character said: 'Let's have some tea, Cowboy.' That teapot was big and heavy and what was inside was hot. Flack knew what was in my mind. 'Fill her up, son,' he said, holding out his can. I gave him a look. He shook his head. So the teapot stayed where it was and nobody had to send for an ambulance. And that was nine o'clock and two hours on, but boy, it felt like two long years to me.

Sid Chaplin The Day of the Sardine

(a) Why does no one notice Arthur? What effect do you think this has on him?
(b) '... a character with a face like a frog'; what does this phrase tell us of Arthur's attitude towards Sprogget?
(c) 'You don't sound it' (that is, like the gaffer's nevvy). Why does Sprogget say this?
(d) What is the attitude of the men towards Arthur while they are taking the mickey? Why do they treat him like this? Is Arthur's reaction to the mickey-taking realistic? Is it sensible? Is it justified? If your answer to any of these questions is 'no' how should he have behaved, in your opinion? Why?
(e) What is Sprogget's aim in his 'bit talk'?
(f) 'Think a bit about yourself, son'; is this a fair comment on Arthur?
(g) What sort of relationship develops between Arthur and Flack?
(h) On the evidence in this passage, what sort of relationship do you think is likely to develop between Arthur and the people he is going to work with?
(i) What elements in Arthur's character do you admire, and which do you dislike? Would you like him for a friend or 'mate'? Why?

Material for further discussion

Spend a few minutes discussing with other members of the class, in small groups, your own experiences of your own first few days at work, and the way *you* were treated. Discuss as well the way you have treated newcomers to the job, or seen them treated, since that time. How did you, and the other newcomers, react? Is it possible to regulate behaviour towards new young entrants to a firm? Such treatment is sometimes called an 'initiation rite'; why? Would you like to see such treatment regulated or stopped altogether, or do you think it is harmless, perhaps even useful? Why? Talk about these and any related issues, then appoint one member of each group to summarize for the rest of the class the conclusions your group has reached.

Drafting a notice

Now suppose that your Site Manager, worried by reports that young workers are having a rough time when they start work, wants to do something to make things easier for them. After discussing the matter with various people, he decides to do two things; first, he will draft a notice laying down rules for employees to observe when young workers start work at the site. He asks you, as a young worker aware of the problems, to help.

Using material from your discussion, but without referring to it directly, draft a notice for the Site Manager to sign; you may find it useful to refer to some recent incident at the site at which you work which makes the notice necessary.

Before drafting the notice discuss where it will be placed and how it can be best designed and phrased to make sure that the employees at the site respond to it. Remember that busy employees don't often bother to read or pay much attention to such material, so how are you going to design it and phrase it so that it is not just ignored? Remember, too, that for the purpose of this exercise you are the Site Manager; what attitude are you going to take? Are you going to dictate to the persons concerned, or to reason with them, to command them, or perhaps appeal to their good sense? Can you, or would you want to do all of these things in one notice?

When they are completed, circulate the notices and try to decide which would be most effective, and which would be ineffective, and why.

Letter writing

(a) Now the Site Manager decides to send a letter to all young entrants to the firm before they start work, giving useful advice on the way he thinks they should behave, the sort of treatment they might expect, and how they should react to it. Again, with your earlier discussion in mind, try to write the letter you might have found useful before you started work. Remember, however, that when the young worker arrives, you, as Site Manager, will be his boss, so try to show in the letter some sign of your authority.
Note: at this stage do not bother much about the conventions of letter-writing – that is, the setting out of the addresses, 'Yours faithfully' and so on; we shall work on these later.

(b) Again using your earlier discussion as a starting point, write a short letter (again ignoring the 'conventions') to the son of a friend of yours who is starting work in the same sort of job you started a few months ago. Give him some information about the sort of problems he is likely to meet and suggest how he should respond to these.
Note: if you can base this on your own experience, perhaps

quoting actual incidents, you will find it easier than trying to make it up.

Discussion work

Finally, if he is at all approachable, show your notice and letters to your own Site Manager or immediate supervisor and ask his opinion about them, and also about the problems of young workers in general, as he sees them. Bring his comments to the class next week. With a collection of such comments available, you could form last week's groups and discuss whether what you wrote then should be in any way altered.

Unit 2

Comprehension (including discussion material)

Read the following passage, and then answer the questions below.

'You go down the site on a freezing cold morning. By nine you are wallowing in mud. The toilets are in a shed if you're lucky. There's no hot water; just a tap. At the end of the day you're soaked to the skin and stiff with cold. You pile into a truck and think of nothing but a hot meal and a bath. After 5
that, there's night school three evenings a week. But it's the only way, and I'm glad I'm doing it.' So said a young builder's apprentice.
   It's tough being an apprentice – but not as tough as it was. Once a lad had to be indentured to one firm for seven long 10
years, while his parents were keeping him at home and also paying his employer a large fee for teaching him a trade. Even today, in some white-collar apprenticeships such as the Law, this archaic practice still survives. But in industry apprenticeship is considered a privilege. 15
   Most apprentices begin like Ernest O'Neill, who won a silver medal in the 1965 International Apprentice Competition for his electric welding. He became an apprentice because there was no alternative. He was determined to make the best of it and now earns £1,000 a year as an instructor. 20
   Like most top apprentices, O'Neill feels a mixture of ambition and content. 'I want to get on' he says, 'and I want to continue studying until I'm twenty-five, and to get my HNC. There's no limit to how far you can go if you're keen and work 25
hard. It's a struggle at first, and there have been times when I've wanted to go home and rest for six weeks, but it's been worth it.'
   Most of the top apprentices lead uncluttered lives. They have to. Few start at more than £4 a week and are lucky if 30
they get £13 at the end of the indentures. Many have to buy their own books and tools.
   Politics bore them. Most of them belong to a trade union, and agree they serve a useful purpose, but play no active part

in them. As apprentices they cannot go on strike nor join in industrial disputes, and this presents problems. As O'Neill says: 'You can't go against the firm and you can't go against the union. You're right up against it.'

Apprenticeship in its present form is probably out of date. Mr Marsh, Parliamentary Secretary to the Ministry of Labour, said: 'We are moving towards a day when a much more general training is needed, when a person will be taught several skills in a lifetime.' At the moment, each of the Boards set up under the Industrial Training Act is working out the kind and length of training it considers suitable for its own industry. The outcome will undoubtedly be a revolution in the quality and numbers of young people choosing a career in industry.

Colin Chapman The Sunday Times

(a) Consider the comments in the first paragraph; discuss with other members of the class how the conditions described compare with the conditions under which you work. What advantages, if any, might a building apprentice have over apprentices in other trades?

(b) Do you think apprenticeship is a privilege? What price, in money and other terms, do you pay for this 'privilege'? Discuss how far you think it is worth the price you pay. Divide into pairs; make one member of each pair responsible for arguing the case for apprenticeship while the other assumes he is not an apprentice and argues against it; **or** one member of the pair assumes he wishes to give up his apprenticeship, while the other takes on the role of his father, who is opposed to his doing so.

(c) O'Neill, the passage says, feels a mixture of ambition and content; is this how you feel about your apprenticeship? If so, ambition for what, and content with what?

(d) Throughout the passage, but particularly in the fifth and sixth paragraphs, the author generalizes about apprentices. Ask other members of the class, and if possible apprentices in other classes, whether they think they fit the picture of apprentices the writer draws. If you do not already know, find out what the word 'stereotype' means, and then be prepared to report back to the rest of the class whether you consider the author is presenting to the reader an accurate account of apprentices in general, or whether he is presenting a misleading stereotype of the apprentice.

(e) This passage was written in 1965. Basing your answer on your own experience, and on that of fellow apprentices, estimate how far the improvements in the system foreseen by Mr. Marsh have been realized.

Critical Work

Many of the statements people make are statements of fact. This means that they can be proved to be true or false. Examples of such statements are: 'In 1978 Ipswich Town beat Arsenal in the FA Cup Final' and 'Huddersfield is in Devon'. The first of these statements is true, the second is false, but they are both statements of fact since their truth or falsity can be proved and so it is pointless to argue about them; if there is disagreement all we can usefully do is to consult someone or some book which will supply the answer.

Other statements, however, although they are often expressed as if they were statements of fact, are really matters of opinion. These are open to argument, since intelligent and well-informed people will often genuinely disagree about them. Examples of such statements are: 'Trade Unions are running this country' and 'Elton John is a better singer than David Bowie'.

In which category – factual statement or statement of opinion – would you place each of the following quotations (or near quotations) from the above passage?
    (a) It's tough being an apprentice (line 9).
    (b) Once a boy had to be indentured to a firm for seven years (line 10).
    (c) ... this archaic principle (that is, paying for apprenticeships) still survives in some white-collar apprenticeships (line 14).
    (d) O'Neill won a silver medal in the 1965 International Apprentice Competition (line 16).
    (e) He now (that is, in 1965) earns £1,000 a year (line 20).
    (f) Most top apprentices lead uncluttered lives (line 29).
    (g) Politics bore them (line 33).
    (h) An apprentice is not allowed to go on strike (line 35).
    (i) The outcome (of The Industrial Training Boards) will undoubtedly be a revolution in the quality and number of young people choosing a career in industry (line 46).

Elementary Research

By using your college library find and copy out ten factual statements about apprenticeship (copy the sentences from at least three different sources, and make a note of the sources). Then copy out from the same or different sources ten statements about apprenticeship which you consider are statements of opinion; again, make a note of the sources. When you return to the classroom, work in pairs and exchange your lists; see whether your partner agrees with your choices and whether you agree with his – if you cannot agree, ask the lecturer to give his decision.

Organization of material

Circulate all the lists throughout the class. As each list reaches you, copy from it any sentences, together with sources, which you could use for the following exercises. Having consulted as many lists as possible, write three paragraphs on **one** aspect of apprenticeship – you should bear this task in mind while collecting your material from the lists so that you won't have to copy too many sentences. In writing your account you may use the exact words of your sources if you wish, but you should link them together in your own words. You need not, of course, use all the material you collect.

At the end of your work, list all the sources the material has come from; such a list is called a **bibliography**.

Unit 3

Comprehension (including discussion material and critical work)

Read Passages A and B; then answer the questions below.

Passage A
We needed a new path round our greenhouse, so I ordered three bags of cement from a local builder. I specified that they should be transported by a small truck, so they could be unloaded *in situ*. But there was a failure of communication. A man turned up with a lorry about a hundred yards long and there was nothing for it but to accept delivery of the cement at the front gate and transport it myself.

By the time I took the third enormous weight on my shoulders and staggered up the path the lorry man had begun to take an interest in my performance. Groaning with rage and pain, I heard him say — and the note of contempt was unmistakable — 'Well, I can see *you* aren't used to humping cement.'

Here was the triumphant voice of the working man, proud of his physical strength and vitality, putting a sedentary middle-aged writer firmly in his place. I have heard this voice before, from farm labourers, who can perform in a few hours a task that would take me weeks.

In my observation, it is a myth that everyone wants a 'cushy' job. A great many men, and not a few women, positively prefer jobs which require physical power and skill. They exult in the resources of their bodies.

I think we should bear in mind this fact, for it is a fact, when we consider the question 'Who should get paid for what?' I sympathise with those who feel that market forces alone should not be allowed to determine the wages and salaries of different jobs and professions. Of course, there should be 'danger money', dirty money', extra pay for unsocial hours and high rates for the jobs nobody in his right mind would want to do.

But, human nature being complex, it does not follow that what constitutes an agreeable job, and what does not, are universally shared. Hence the modern proposition, held by some theorists of a social wages policy, that work should be rewarded by inverse ratio to its acceptability, cannot be made to function, since there is no agreement on 'nice' and 'nasty' jobs.

Paul Johnson *Sunday Telegraph Magazine*

Passage B
On the lump you couldn't straighten your back from one end of the day to the other. You had to get a sub every day for a drink just to get the sweat back into your body.
  It was pure slavery. You have no right to notice, they can sack you on the spot. If you have an accident on the lump you get nothing. Instead of getting benefit, they probably discover you haven't been paying tax or buying stamps and you get prosecuted.
  When you work you have a pacemaker in front of you who gets £4 more than you and you have to keep up with him. You look for bricklayers' jobs in the paper and it says 'greyhounds only,' meaning speed merchants. But we're not dogs, we're human beings.
  It increases unemployment fantastically. Four men do 20 men's work. And when you're over 45 you're finished completely.
  There's a non-union site next to us. There are no proper eating facilities, no washing facilities, nowhere to change your clothes. Men have to keep a change of clothes in cardboard boxes, in the middle of the site, where rain can get at them.

Socialist Worker

Questions on Passage A

(a) What was the lorry man contemptuous of (line 11)?
(b) How would you explain his 'triumphant voice' (line 13)?
(c) When the author says (line 15) that he has heard this voice before, he obviously doesn't mean that he has heard this man speak before; what, then, does he mean?
(d) The writer says (line 18) that it is a 'myth' that everyone wants a cushy job; what is the literal meaning of the word 'myth'? (If you don't know what 'literal' means look it up in a dictionary.) What does the word 'myth' mean in this passage? What connection is there between the two meanings?
(e) Why do you think the author felt it necessary to insert the phrase 'for it is a fact' (line 22)?
(f) What does the writer mean when, in line 24, he refers to 'market forces'? How might they determine wages and salaries?

(g) Define 'danger money', 'dirty money', 'unsocial hours'; give a few examples of jobs for which money is paid for each of these.
(h) What sort of jobs do you think the author has in mind when he talks about 'jobs that nobody in their right minds would want to do' (line 28)?
(i) The passage quoted is part of a longer article. The paragraph immediately following the extract quoted begins with the word 'But . . .'. Write a short paragraph beginning with the word 'But . . .' developing the argument as you think the author might have developed it.

Questions on Passage B

(a) What evidence does the author give in the passage that the job was 'pure slavery'? Are you convinced by the evidence? Why?
(b) Why does the author say 'But we are not dogs'? What is he suggesting about the employers, and for what reasons? Do you think, on the evidence of the passage, it is a fair suggestion?
(c) Would you include the work described here in your list in the answer to question (h) on Passage A? If so, why do people do it?
(d) You have almost certainly been told that in your writing you should not use the word 'you' to mean 'anybody', 'somebody' and so on; yet the author of this passage does so throughout the passage. Try to rewrite the first three paragraphs of this passage without using the word 'you'. Circulate all the attempts and decide whether any of them are as effective as the original. If you decide they are, does this mean that the authors are writing poor English? If, however, you decide that the original is better (perhaps more forceful) than any produced by the class, does this mean that the advice you have been given – to avoid using the word 'you' – is pointless and can be ignored? Discuss this with your lecturer.

Questions on both passages.

(a) In Passage A Paul Johnson seems to be saying that physical work can be satisfying. In Passage B the author deplores the physical strain imposed on the workers he is describing. Does this mean that the two authors disagree?
(b) When we write we usually have a particular reader, or

particular type of reader in mind. When the authors were writing these passages, what sort of reader(s) do you think they had in mind? Is it likely that anyone reading Passage A with interest would find Passage B equally interesting? Or are they likely to appeal to quite different types of readers? Try to give reasons for your answer by finding in the passages phrases or sentences which you think might appeal to certain types of reader, or which might make some readers throw the passage away with disgust or boredom. Which of the following, for example, might be interested in either or both passages: a foreman on a building site; a building trade unionist; a lecturer in civil engineering; a lecturer in English; a van driver; a doctor; your father; your girl friend?

(c) What effect do you think the authors of each of these passages hope to have on their readers? Do they hope to make them think, to change their attitudes, to inform them of something they did not know, to entertain them? They might, of course, be hoping to do several of these things at the same time, and maybe other things too, which you can add to the list.

Material for further discussion

(a) In Passage A the author refers to people 'exulting in the resources of their bodies'. What sports or pastimes can you think of to which the phrase might be applied? What is their appeal?

or

Concentrate on one activity and suggest why some people, perhaps including yourself, find it pleasurable.

(b) Work in groups. Make a list of any jobs which all members of your group agree are 'cushy'; try to decide individually whether you would like to do any of these jobs (assuming you were trained and capable of doing them). If you would not, why do you consider such jobs 'cushy'? Can you find any job that everyone in the class thinks is 'cushy'? If so, try during the next week to find out if it has any disadvantages. Do you think someone might honestly call the job you do 'cushy'?

Unit 4

Note-taking and expansion of notes

1 and 2 below are accounts of accidents. In 1, the opening of the report is given in full, the ending has been reduced to note form; in 2, the opening is given in note form, the ending in the words of the original.

1. A workman who had gone onto a ridged roof to renew some slates was seriously injured when the crawling board he was using slipped down the 30° slope and he fell about 15 feet. The board, which was about 9 feet long by 8 inches wide, had a 3-inch block fixed to one end as an anchor over the ridge of the roof, but as he moved on the board it slipped off.

   Width board too narrow.
   Anchor blocks – not deep enough for any roof. HERE risk increased; very heavy ridged roof tiles → upper part of board clear of surface.
   Man steps on this part of board → board bends downwards, anchor block off roof tiles.
   Board used frequently on this type roof ∴ permanent warp ∴ not flat on any surface.

2. Two carpenters renew shutter cord in paper mill.
   Shutter covered roof light.
   Roof – asbestos-cement; saw-toothed.
   Decided could best be done from outside.
   Access – over 2 bays; crawling board used; permanently in place.

   They then walked along the valley gutter alongside the roof where the work was. The gutter was narrow, and as the men walked along, carrying a crawling board between them, one of them either slipped or misjudged his footing and fell onto the asbestos-cement sheeting, through which he fell to the floor of the shop below.
   B. A. C. Whyte *Safety on the Site*

(a) Complete each of the reports in the style of the original.
(b) Reduce each of the accounts to note form throughout.

Comprehension and critical work

The following passages are extracts from *Hazards of Work* by Patrick Kinnersly, published by Pluto Press. Read them, and then answer the questions following.

1 If you work a lifetime in industry you can expect to have at least one serious injury that will keep you off work for more than three days. If you work in the construction industry you can expect three or four before you retire, if you live that long. One in 50 building workers dies in an accident on site.

2 The significant fact about this accident (failure of a riveter's staging which sent a worker falling 180 feet to his death) which would not be considered in a Factory Inspector's report is that the riveters are paid by the hundred rivets, not for the time it takes to put up the staging. Needless to say, they try to put up the staging in the least possible time.

3 'Ideally, the company would have liked to have had an arrangement whereby the whole length would have been scaffolded. But this was out of the question because of the expense.' Mr Green, of Babcock and Wilcox, giving evidence after the death of a welder. The decision to skimp on safe access and a proper guard rail cost it a fine of just £600. In 1970 Babcock and Wilcox made a profit of more than £3 million.

4 'Mr Peel, for the company, said that if the regulations regarding the shoring-up of trenches were rigidly enforced there would be thousands of prosecutions a day. There would have been no prosecution now if there had not been an accident. He added that the contractors would find many jobs impracticable if they shored earthworks as thoroughly as regulations demanded.' A man had been injured in a trench collapse; the firm was fined £50.

(a) In one sentence, state what effect you think the writer hopes passage 1 will have on the reader.
(b) In 2, why does the author say the fact is 'significant'?
(c) In 2, why would this 'significant fact' not be considered by a Factory Inspector? What might the writer be suggesting about the usefulness of the Factory Acts?

(d) In 2, what, according to the author, was (i) the immediate, and (ii) the real cause of the accident?
(e) In 3, does the author consider the fine too high, too little, or about fair? How does he indicate his opinion to the reader?
(f) Does the defence offered by Mr. Green seem adequate to you (passage 3)? Does it seem adequate to the author? In each case, try to explain how you arrive at your conclusions.
(g) In 3, we are told that the firm's profits were more than £3 million – and this is a statement of fact; it is not open to argument (look back at the Critical Work you did on this in Unit 2). And yet there is little doubt that it is intended to be part of the argument. How does the author expect us to see it as part of the argument?
(h) In 4, what does 'economically impracticable' mean?
(i) 'There would have been no prosecution now if there had not been an accident' (passage 4). By quoting this the writer is making a similar point to one he has made in one of the other passages; what is that point?
(j) On the evidence of all these passages, what would you say is the chief object of Mr. Kinnersly in writing the book? Is he, in your opinion, being fair, or is he biased? If you consider he is biased, how does this bias appear, since he does no more than make statements of fact, which must be accurate (if they were not, he could be sued for libel)?

Work on statistics

The figures below are extracts from an official table showing numbers and causes of accidents in the construction industry during 1973.

	Building operations		Works of engineering construction	
	Fatal	Total	Fatal	Total
Falls of persons	89	8760	9	1397
From height	87	5707	8	696
On the flat	2	2053	1	701
Falls of material (other than in excavations and tunnelling)	13	2231	3	568
From height	9	1690	3	387
On the flat	4	541	–	181

Excavations	6	89	17	162
Burial by fall of material	4	32	13	65
Struck my material from side (other than burial)	2	57	4	97
Tunnelling	–	23	2	52
Burial by fall of material	–	4	2	2
Struck by material from side (other than burial)	–	19	–	48
Lifting equipment	15	467	11	254
Hoists				
Fall of platform or cage	1	26	1	1
Trapping by hoist	2	50	–	3
Cranes and other appliances (including falls of persons and materials)	12	354	10	246
Machinery	2	1172	1	613

HM Inspector of Factories' Report, 1974; Appendix 7

The following ten statements refer to the table above. You are asked to decide, for each statement, whether, according to figures given, it is true, whether it is false, or whether there is insufficient evidence for you to say whether it is true or false. If you decide that there is insufficient evidence, try to decide what evidence you would need before deciding whether that particular statement is true or false.

  1 It is safer to work on works of engineering construction than on building operations.
  2 At least 5% of deaths due to falls shown in the table resulted from people falling while on the flat.
  3 The total number of people killed and injured by falling material was less than 2,800.
  4 These figures show how careless construction workers are.
  5 Roughly one construction worker is killed for every 150 construction accidents reported.
  6 Tunnelling is safer work than work on excavations.
  7 These figures show an appalling lack of safety precautions on building sites.
  8 More than a third of the accidents caused by lifting equipment were due to use of cranes and other appliances.

9 There were fewer than 100 accidents reported due to burial by fall of material during tunnelling operations.
10 The figures for tunnelling and excavation suggest that in this type of work construction workers are more careful than employees of engineering construction firms.

(a) When does an accident have to be reported? If you don't know, try to find out.
(b) Why are such figures as these published? (Try to give more than one reason.) Who might make use of them, and how?
(c) These figures relate to 1973. Look in your college library to find figures for a more recent year. If there are any significant differences, list them and try to explain them.
(d) Only part of the table is reproduced here; what other causes of accidents on building sites do you think might be included?
(e) Try to find out how many accidents were reported from your place of work last year; also try to find out what categories they came into. Did they fall into roughly the same pattern as is shown in this table? If not, can you suggest reasons for this?

Narrative Report

All accidents at work causing injury have to be notified. In most cases these official reports are filed and forgotten, but any one of them could become very important, since there could be an argument about who was to blame, and the report may be presented as evidence in court. If, therefore, you do have to write an accident report (and the likelihood is that you will, some day) make sure before you sign it that you have given all the relevant details you can think of, as accurately as you can.

In order to gain some practice in writing such a report, arrange for one member of your class who has been involved in, or witnessed, an accident at work to answer questions about it from the rest of the class; he should give no information except in answer to questions. The class should try to draw from him, by asking the right questions, a full account of what happened, and should take notes of the answers he gives; then, working in groups, sort out the information into logical order before writing a report under relevant headings.

The report should:
(a) state who it is written for. Head your report 'For the attention of Safety Officer, Moors Construction Ltd';

(b) have a formal heading – for example, 'Report of an Accident on Dobbins's Building Site, West Street, Welshbury';
(c) state date, time, place and nature of the accident;
(d) give a clear account of what happened as you experienced it; remember, no two people see an accident in exactly the same way, so your account may be challenged; so be as precise as you can but be as sure as you can that your details are accurate – the sooner you write your report, the more sure you can be;
(e) include in this section the names of any witnesses;
(f) state what action you and anyone else took as a result of the accident;
(g) if possible, suggest how the risk of such an accident occurring again can be reduced or removed;
(h) sign and date it when you are sure, after reading it through, that you have said, accurately, all you need to say.
(j) You should *not* say whose fault it was; this is not your concern and it may get you into trouble.

Unit 5

Multiple Choice Comprehension

In previous comprehension exercises, both in this book and, probably, in the work you used to do at school, you have been asked to write out, often in complete sentences, answers to questions on the passage set. There is, however, another method of testing whether you have understood what you have read; it is called multiple choice testing and it is used in other subjects as well as in English. The first exercise in this chapter is of this type, and you will find several other exercises of this type later in the book. Before you attempt it, you may find the following advice useful.

Each multiple choice question presents four or five options, only one of which is correct. Read each item carefully before deciding which is the correct one, and do not jump to conclusions. What is being tested is your ability to read with understanding, to think, and to select. To reach the correct solution requires knowledge based on understanding; it also requires care.

Some incorrect options, or 'distractors' as they are sometimes called, may be very nearly but not quite correct; others may be traps for the careless; you should, therefore, consider each of the options very carefully before deciding which is the correct one. You will not get marks for 'near misses'.

Certain items you may well find you can answer by *elimination*, that is, by deciding that three of the four (or four of the five) options *must* be wrong, so the other must be correct. Even if you can eliminate only two or three of the options as being obviously wrong you will be in a position to make an intelligent guess at which, among those remaining, is the correct answer. In any event, do not leave any of the questions unanswered – you will not lose any marks if your guess is wrong, and it may be correct.

Read the passage below, and then for each of the questions following write down the letter which you think indicates the correct answer.

Good brick is unlike concrete and stucco in needing no maintenance or surface treatment. It is improved by weathering and even looks the better for the passage of 500 years. It is often more durable than natural stone. The London stock and yellow gault bricks with which Joseph Bazalgette built the great sewers of London between 1858 and 1875 continue to serve their purpose. Concrete has been tried in recent times for sewer work, but bricks have been shown to wear better under the scouring of miscellaneous fluids and grit, and to form stronger and more satisfactory junctions and to be less slippery for the sewer men to walk on.

The handy weight and shape makes brick relatively untiring to build with, for the workman can grasp the brick with one hand while picking up mortar with the other; he finds it, too, a flexible unit with which to follow most drawings. Even in the great stone building areas of the Mediterranean, it may be seen again and again in older houses that window and doorway arches, set like raised eyebrows in the stonework, are neatly and strongly brick. However, the extent to which builders have turned to bricks because of their regularity is traditionally hidden by a stucco finish (there are plenty of houses in the old quarters of Paris which contain less of the local coarse limestone than at first appears).

Having been hardened by intense heat, bricks are very good at resisting fire. Thus the metal in steel-framed buildings may be buried for safety in brickwork; and the flues and chimney stacks of old houses, stone as well as wooden, are often brick. Few bricks lack toughness, but obviously some must be used with common sense. There are less than fully-fired bricks which should not be exposed, unrendered, in the outer leaf of a wall; the otherwise robust fletton bricks are damaged by frost if laid as a coping on parapets.

But in general, where brickwork has failed in any respect, the fault is unlikely to be in the bricks themselves. Take the damp patch on a ground-floor wall of a country cottage. This could well be explained by the absence of a dampcourse or the presence just outside of a banked-up flower bed. If chimney breasts upstairs are damp, the cause could lie in a lack of flashing at the junction of stack and roof.

It has never been a protection against rain to build with the hardest, densest bricks, for wherever water has encouragement to get in, it does so through chinks in the mortar joints rather than through the bricks themselves. In fact, bricks that are porous enough to absorb a certain amount of water actually discourage the entry of rain at the joints.

J. Woodforde *Bricks to Build a House*

1 Which one of the following statements, according to the passage, is true?
  A All brickwork needs surface treatment.
  B No brickworks needs maintenance.
  C Good stucco does not need maintenance.
  D Good brickwork needs no maintenance or surface treatment.
2 Which one of the following is stated or implied by the author?
  A After 500 years brickwork begins to deteriorate.
  B Stonework is not improved by weathering.
  C Only after 500 years does brick look better than stone.
  D Good brickwork lasts longer than stonework.
3 'Miscellaneous' (line 9) means
  A liable to attack the brickwork
  B of several different types
  C unpleasant
  D harmful
4 'Relatively untiring' (line 12) means
  A very tiring
  B very tiring at times
  C less tiring than working with other materials
  D less tiring to the mind than to the body
5 Which one of the following is *not* stated to be a specific advantage of brickwork for sewers?
  A Concrete does not wear as well as brick under scouring.
  B Concrete is more slippery than brick to walk on.
  C Bricks are particularly untiring to work with when constructing sewers.
  D Joints between the sections are more satisfactory in brickwork than in concrete.
6 'Flexible' (line 15) means
  A easy to understand
  B easy to manipulate in different circumstances
  C adapted to hold in the hand
  D adapted for following the drawing
7 In the second paragraph the author suggests that something is surprising. This is that
  A the doorways and arches in the Mediterranean area are strongly built
  B brick is a flexible unit
  C in the Mediterranean area, most building is of stone
  D doorways and arches of stone buildings in the Mediterranean area are made of brick

8 The metal in steel-framed buildings may be buried in brickwork because it is
   A strong and will support the bricks
   B less likely than bricks to be affected by fire
   C more likely than bricks to be affected by damp
   D needed to harden the bricks
9 'Unrendered' (line 30) means
   A not covered by another material
   B without sufficient mortar
   C unpolished
   D unprotected
10 The author explains the possible reasons for damp on ground floors and in chimney breasts
   A so that we do not think they result from poor quality bricks
   B because it is useful for the reader to know these facts in case they should occur in his own home
   C to warn the reader against employing poor workmen
   D because they indicate two different results of using poor quality bricks
11 'Flashing' (line 39) means
   A use of special mortar to protect a joint in brickwork
   B protection of a joint in brickwork by covering it with a continuous metal strip
   C insertion of a special form of decoration
   D use of a specially shaped brick
12 The main point that the author is making in the fifth paragraph is
   A porous brick should be used whenever possible
   B it is rare for any brick to let in water
   C the hardest, densest brick should normally be used
   D it is common fault for bricklayers to leave chinks in the mortar joints
13 Which of the following statements best sums up what the author is saying in this passage?
   A Bricks are the very best building material ever devised.
   B The disadvantages of brick for building are outweighed by its advantages.
   C Buildings of brick have too many likely faults for us to class brick as the ideal building material.
   D Bricks are a very good building material.

14 Which one of the following statements is *not* contradicted in the passage?
  A There are many brick buildings which we do not recognize as being of brick.
  B Because all bricks are tough, it does not much matter which sort are used.
  C Concrete has been used for building sewers, but more recently bricks have been found more effective.
  D Often when rain comes into a house, it is because poor quality brick, or the wrong type of brick has been used.
15 The passage was most probably written for
  A someone studying for a qualification as a builder
  B a person who owns, or is thinking of buying, his own house, and is a keen do-it-yourself man
  C a student of architecture
  D a reader who has no specialized knowledge or practical interest in the matter

Research and organization of material

The following might form the plan for an article on brick manufacture:
1. Obtaining the material:–
   (a) Clay.
   (b) Brick earths.
   (c) Other materials.
2. Its preparation for use:–
   (a) Weathering.
   (b) Tempering.
3. Moulding to shapes: methods:–
   (a) Slop moulding.
   (b) Soft plastic moulding.
   (c) Soft plastic pressing.
   (d) Wire cutting.
   (e) Stiff plastic pressing.
   (f) Dry pressing.
4. Drying:–
   (a) Natural drying.
   (b) Artificial drying.
5. Firing:–
   (a) Reasons for firing.
   (b) Methods of firing.
      (i) Clamp burning.
      (ii) Intermittent kilns.
      (iii) Continuous kilns.

For this exercise work in pairs, each pair taking one of the sections listed above. By using the college library and/or any other resources, find out as much as you can about your section, and write it up together, in a form that would be suitable to form part of a chapter of a textbook on brick manufacture (*note*: use at least two sources and make a note of them).

When you have completed this, exchange your material with one of the other pairs. Read through what they have written, and underline anything which you do not fully understand; also, be prepared to ask them for further information which you think is necessary or which would be relevant.

Each pair should then rewrite the original draft, incorporating the amendments and additions requested, using further resource material if necessary.

The final versions can then be stapled together to form a continuous account of brick manufacture. Add at the end a bibliography specifying details of all sources used.

Research

By consulting reference books, draw up a table showing the special characteristics, including their qualities and limitations, and the main uses of the following types of brick:
Fletton, Accrington, Staffordshire, Rubber, London stocks.

Discussion

In his novel *Bleak House*, written about 130 years ago, Dickens described a visit to the cottage of a brickmaker and his family. Try to find a copy of the novel and read that description (it is near the end of Chapter 8) and discuss with the rest of the class what you think Dickens was trying to tell the reader in this description. You might wish to consider some of the following questions – though not necessarily in the order in which they are given: what is the attitude of the brickmaking community in general towards the visitors? How does the narrator's attitude towards the brickmakers differ from the attitude of Mrs. Pardiggle? Does Dickens, do you think, have any sympathy for the brickmaker? What is the effect, do you think, on the brickmaker, of Mrs. Pardiggle's comment that she is fond of hard work? What is the brickmaker trying to tell Mrs. Pardiggle – and the others – in his long speech, beginning 'Then make it easy for her!'?

Unit 6

Comprehension and summarizing

Read the following passage; then answer the questions below.

During the past 50 years timber has passed from being one of the cheapest and most easily obtainable of all building materials to one which is expensive and in short supply. This is the inevitable result of an almost criminally wasteful misuse of resources in the main timber-producing countries, where forests have been ruthlessly cleared, with little attempt to replant, and of a lack of foresight in the importing countries, such as Britain, where a determined afforestation policy during the period between the wars would have made it possible to meet something like 95 per cent of our present requirements of softwoods from home production. As it is, timber has been increasingly pricing itself out of the market for 25 years, and, for constructional uses, it must now in many countries be considered almost a luxury material.

Against this background, the consumption of timber for building purposes during the previous centuries appears almost unbelievably prodigal. It is useful to work out an approximate cost, at today's prices, of the oak used in the construction of the half-timbered houses common in England in the 15th, 16th and 17th centuries. If it could be obtained in the sizes, shapes and quality needed, the oak for the framing and roof-timber of a modest sized farmhouse would nowadays cost at least £20,000 (at 1973 prices). What was once the commonest of building materials has now become an expensive imported luxury and modern architects do everything possible to avoid using it.

For the whole of the 18th and 19th centuries timber seemed inexhaustible in the USA, and it was felled, used and exported in what now seems the most wasteful and reckless fashion. It remained the dominant material for industrial and railway structures until the middle of the 19th century. Large elaborate timber bridges were being constructed in the USA as late as the 1850's, with ingenious trusses to enable very heavy loads to be taken across rivers and ravines. The techniques evolved for these timber trusses were later transferred to steel, so that many American bridges of the second half of the century had a timber look about them.

K. Hudson *Building Materials*

(a) Explain the meaning of each of the following words and phrases as used in the passage: 'almost criminally wasteful use of resources'; 'a determined afforestation policy'; 'timber has been increasingly pricing itself out of the market'; 'prodigal'; 'the dominant material'.
(b) What are softwoods? How do they differ from hardwoods? Give a few examples of each and explain how their uses differ.
(c) What is a half-timbered building? Can you think of any reason(s) why they were so popular at the times mentioned? Try to find an example of a half-timbered building in your area. Some – usually expensive – houses today are half-timbered; why should people who can afford to buy expensive houses want to use a technique that is no longer necessary or appropriate?
(d) In the second paragraph the author is not saying that the wood used in a half-timbered house built 300–500 years ago would have cost £20,000; what exactly is he saying?
(e) What does the author mean when he says that wood is now considered in many countries a luxury material? Can you suggest some examples in modern house-building where wood is used largely as a luxury? Can you suggest – or find – examples in recent buildings of parts of a house which were traditionally made of wood but which are now normally made of other materials?
(f) Suppose that members of your class are to compile a project on 'How Building Materials are Changing', and you have elected to write the section on wood. You have discovered the above extract and would like to use some of the ideas in it for your introductory paragraph, but as your contribution to the project is to be limited to 700 words, it will have to be compressed.
  (i) Write the opening paragraph of your contribution, based on the above material but using no more than 150 words. You will not be able to use all the material, so decide what are the most important points for your purpose and rearrange them to suit your purpose. Write in your own words (you will need to do this to keep within the length required) in the main, but you may quote the author if you think anything he says is so important that it is vital to use his words; but in this case don't forget to use quotation marks.
  (ii) Decide how you would want your contribution to continue, and use the college library to find relevant information. Write the second paragraph of your con-

tribution based on material that you have found, but again selected and shortened from a piece of longer material. Again, it should not be longer than 150 words. At the end of both paragraphs quote the sources you have used as part of your bibliography.

Technical writing: definitions

Chisels are classified according to their use.

Firmer chisels are the jack planes of the chisels. They may be used for light mortising, chopping out, paring, and all work for which a chisel is required. They are obtainable in widths from 3mm to 50mm.

Mortise chisels are stouter than firmer chisels so that they can withstand the heavy mallet blows and levering necessary when a joiner is making large and deep mortises. They are obtainable in widths from 2mm to 25mm.

Bevelled edge chisels are bevelled on each side and are thus for dovetailing and working into corners. They are obtainable in sizes from 3mm to 50mm.

Paring chisels are, in fact, long bevelled edge chisels, and are used for cleaning deep mortises, stop chamfering, and so on. The joiner normally only has one paring chisel, 25mm or 35mm wide.

Gouges
Gouges may be defined as curved chisels, and are mainly used for shaping, carving and scribing. They are ground on the inside for scribing, and on the outside for shaping and carving.
 The grinding of gouges is usually carried out on a grinding wheel. For inside-ground gouges a wheel profiled to the shape of the gouge is necessary, but for outside-ground gouges a flat wheel is necessary. Finger slip stones are necessary for the purpose. These have two curved edges to suit all sizes of gouge.

R. Bayliss *Carpentry and Joinery*

(a) From the passage above make a list of the words used that would only be fully understood by someone used to working with wood.

(b) Try to define each of these words in such a way that someone unfamiliar with working with wood would know exactly what they mean. When you have done this, try to find someone who does know very little about woodwork and ask him (or her) if he can understand the word from your definition. If he says he does, try to devise a test which would check whether he has understood or not (if it proves that he has not understood properly, this doesn't mean that he was lying – we all, from time to time, think we understand something when we do not). Keep on trying to define each of the terms until each is understood, or at least until it is clear that it will not be understood. Then, in class, try to work out in discussion what the difficulties are in trying to define something for someone who has no knowledge of the matter to begin with.

(c) Choose any five simple tools and define them as accurately as you can, but in each case **omit the name of the tool being defined**. Keep your definition as short as possible – about as long as a dictionary definition would be. Change papers with a classmate and ask him if he can state precisely what five tools are being defined. For any of those that are not recognized accurately, don't tell him what the tool is, but try to improve your definition – and continue to do so until it is accurate enough for him to recognize it. In each case, discuss with each other what was lacking in the definitions that failed.

Vocabulary

During the next week try to find from any source (for example: notes from your technical lecturers, shop window notices, newspapers, advertisement hoardings, books) examples of the following words. Copy out the sentences in which they occur and bring them to class next week. Bring more than one example of each if you can. For future reference you will be asked to copy down accurately all the examples that are produced.

List of words:
loose; lose: its; it's:
whether; weather: waste; waist:
effect; affect: past; passed.

Unit 7

Comprehension with research

Read the following passage; then answer the questions below.

Lafarge, the French makers of high alumina cement (HAC), now state that in all cases of collapse in Britain, the firms which designed, cast and used the concrete are at fault, not the material. All that is needed is a strict list of rules governing its use. The report claims that the engineering and construction companies got their quantities of water and cement wrong, used the wrong aggregates, or allowed the cement to be used in buildings where it was likely to be attacked by chemicals from other structural components. Or the cement took the blame for failures of other factors of construction, such as corroding pre-tensioning wires in concrete.

Evidence collected by Lafarge says that none of the British incidents can be directly attributable to HAC alone, even though in certain cases the chemical change known as 'conversion' was taking place in the material. Indeed, conversion is a stage that concrete passes through to become a stable material.

The key point in the report is that the paramount importance of keeping to the correct water and cement ratios when manufacturing HAC has not always been appreciated. The perfect HAC mix is one in which the water–cement ratio is lower than 0.4 and where there is a minimum cement content of 400 kilograms in every cubic metre.

After the roof-collapses at the Camden and John Cass Schools and Leicester University, British building regulations were changed virtually to exclude HAC. The BSI has also changed its code of practice; any engineer wishing to use HAC 'must rely entirely on his own engineering judgment'. The report attacks the move as negative thinking. 'It would have been more appropriate to concentrate on giving the most conservative guidance, requiring HAC to be designed on the basis of minimum converted strengths, and specifying a maximum instead of a minimum cement content.'

French laws demand that aggregates that attack the concrete may not be used; water–cement ratios must be less than 0.4 and minimum cement content should be at least 400 kilograms per cubic metre; well-constructed shuttering must be used to control setting; premature drying of the concrete must be prevented by removing shuttering early (normally four hours after concrete is placed) and spraying with water for 48 hours.

40

Philip Jordan *The Guardian*

(a) Explain to someone who knows nothing about building what each of the following terms means: aggregates (line 7); pre-tensioning (line 11); conversion (line 14–15); converted strengths (line 32); shuttering (line 37).

(b) Explain to someone who knows nothing about building the meaning of the phrase 'the water–cement ratio is less than 0.4' (line 21).

(c) What point is the author making in the last sentence of the second paragraph?

(d) What is the effect of BSI declaring that any engineer wishing to make use of HAC 'must rely entirely on his own engineering judgment'? What do you assume would have been the situation previously?

(e) The French report says that the BSI should have concentrated on 'giving the most conservative guidance'; what does this mean?

(f) What dangers are guarded against by the precautions outlined in the last paragraph?

(g) The French firm felt that reaction in England to the failures in constructions in which HAC was used was unjustified. Try to find out what conclusions were reached when the collapses were investigated in Britain (they took place in 1973). Discuss with your technology staff how, when such differences arise, they might be resolved.

(h) Suppose that you have been asked to write a short article on HAC which will be handed to next year's students, and which will be sufficiently detailed for them to use as a reference sheet. Use as many sources as possible to write the article, which should contain answers to the following questions (although not necessarily in the order in which they are given) as well as additional information which you think might be useful, interesting or helpful.

Questions to which answers should appear in your article: In what sort of construction work is HAC most useful? Where is it less useful? Where should it not be used at all? When was it first invented? Why is it called 'high alumina cement'? What advantages does it have over other cements? How is it different from other cements? Does it possess any advantage for the client, as distinct from the builder?

At the conclusion add a bibliography.

Organization of material

Below is some information on the routine procedure for testing the strength of concrete. The description is accurate, but the order of the sentences has been jumbled. Working in groups, try to reassemble them in their correct order – your account should then fall naturally into two paragraphs. *Note*: there is no need to alter any of the words, or the order of the words within each sentence.

Appoint one member of the group to keep notes of the discussion so that he can explain afterwards to the rest of the class how his group was able to decide on the correct order; he should note particularly any words or phrases which serve as clues to link sentences to the sentences preceding.

More slender prisms are free to fail naturally without the same restraining effects from the loading plates.

The reason for this is that in practical use the failure of concrete in compression is closely related to induced lateral strains.

They are then crushed between the two horizontal plates of the testing machine.

This arrangement is important because the top surface could only be finished off with a trowel during casting.

For this reason, in many countries a cylindrical test specimen (150mm in diameter by 300mm) is preferred.

They are produced in cast-iron moulds, machined to accurate dimensions.

Such lateral expansion of the concrete is restrained by the loading plates of the testing machine, particularly in units as stocky as cubes.

At the laboratory, before being tested they are arranged so that the side which was on top while the cube was being cast is now vertical.

Cubes are chosen because this is a convenient and compact shape for casting, storing and handling.

However, experiments have shown that, when crushed in this manner, cubes of concrete frequently withstand the test better than the identical material would have done if it were tested in the shape of a beam or a column.

Consequently, it is not as true as the five faces which have been formed by being compressed against the sides of the mould.

Now go back to the exercise you wrote in exercise (h) of the Comprehension section in this chapter. Rewrite your article, jumbling the sentences but making no other alterations, then hand it to a colleague to reassemble as he thinks you originally wrote it. If he can do this without much difficulty, your article was well structured and well organized; if he cannot, discuss with him how it might be improved.

Punctuation and spelling

Rewrite the following passage, punctuating it and correcting all spelling errors. To help you – you should have, when you have finished, eight full stops (including the one at the end of the passage). If you are in doubt whether at any point you should use a full stop or comma, try reading it aloud to someone, or even better, into a tape recorder. If your voice falls when you pause, use a full stop, but if it rises use a comma.

Concrete quickly became a favorite matterial with modern arkiteks but in one sense it did not achieve its full potential untill the advent of Le Corbusier before his work made an impact architecs were obsessed with the notion that in a machine age all buildings should look as though they were made by machine consequently even those which have been labouriously and lovelingly made by hand where plastered over sometimes even painted to give the impression that they had been produced by machine Le Corbusier decided that this was disshonest and felt that the teckneek for making concrete in stead of being hidden should be revealed openly even stressed in the apperaence of a building since concrete is made in molds the form of the mold unless it is deliberatly conceeled will remain when the mold is removed Le Corbusier as a matter of principal decided that for his molds he would use rough wooddan blocks arranged in patterns so that the concrete emmerged as a uneek material conveying an impresion of great strength because the positioning of the boards of the mold did not require great accuracy this method had the additional advantage of ecconomy since fewer skilled workmen were required the method was quickly reconised as an innovation of great significance and many arkiteks visited the sight so many that at times they seriously intefered with the work.

Unit 8

Comprehension

Read the following passage, and then answer the questions below.

The etiquette of the building site came under scrutiny when a young woman who intends to become a trained bricklayer claimed that she had been sacked for swearing on the site, and that this was a discriminatory act.

Janet Krangel, aged 23, was sacked after two months' work 5 on a building site after she swore at the boss of the construction firm for which she worked during a row over her pay packet.

Madeline Colvin, representing Ms Krangel, told the tribunal that Mr Taylor, the boss of the firm, was not a man 10 given to swearing. But, she claimed, he would have tolerated swearing in a man, but not in a woman. 'Maybe he felt it was graceless.' Miss Colvin said that her client and a woman friend who had also worked on the site had joined in the kind of language used on the site and they used swearing as a 15 'means of articulation'.

Ms Krangel was dismissed in July, 1976, after she had said to Mr Taylor, 'You———bastard, you just don't care.' This occurred during a disagreement over holiday pay, to which Ms Krangel thought she was entitled. Mr Taylor denies dis- 20 crimination, and says he did not dismiss Ms Krangel because she could not do the work – 'The foreman says she did it reasonably well' – but because she had sworn at him. Mr Taylor said he had been called a lot of names in his time, but could not recall being abused in the terms Ms Krangel had 25 used.

Ms Krangel had been unable to get jobs on other sites because, it was claimed, of the discrimination against women in the construction industry. She claimed that her dismissal had adversely affected her prospects for further work in the 30 industry and her application to become a skilled bricklayer – for which on-site experience is required.

Mr Taylor said he could not be guilty of discrimination because he had taken on another woman during the same period, had employed Ms Krangel in the first place and had 35 not sacked her after a token number of days. But Miss Colvin claimed that there was 'very strong evidence' that people had never before been dismissed just for swearing.

The tribunal reserved its judgment.

Lynn Owen *The Guardian*

(a) What is meant by each of the following words?
    (i) etiquette (line 1);
    (ii) tolerated (line 11);
    (iii) graceless (line 13.
(b) What is meant by each of the following phrases?
    (i) came under scrutiny (line 1);
    (ii) given to swearing (line 11);
    (iii) a means of articulation (lines 15–16);
    (iv) adversely affected her prospects (line 30).
(c) Explain each of the following:
    (i) a discriminatory act (line 4);
    (ii) the tribunal (lines 9–10);
    (iii) her client (line 13);
    (iv) on-site experience (line 32);
    (v) a token number (line 36).
(d) (i) On what grounds did Ms Krangel claim that she had been unfairly dismissed?
    (ii) What was Mr Taylor's case for dismissing Ms Krangel?
(e) (i) What was the result of the tribunal?
    (ii) What would you expect the final judgment of the tribunal to have been? Why?

Critical work

Obviously, journalists cannot report every fact in a situation, but sometimes they are accused of misrepresenting an issue by carefully selecting which facts they will report, and which they will ignore. The following pieces of information were not mentioned in the report from which the Comprehension passage is an extract (although they were mentioned in a later report in the same paper when the Tribunal's findings were announced). State how relevant you think each of the following pieces of information is, and whether you think, that, by omitting any of them, the journalist gave the reader a false impression of the situation.

(a) Ms Krangel had a good honours degree.
(b) The employer paid lower wages than most other comparable firms in the area.

(c) No one explained to Ms Krangel that employees only get week-in-hand pay when they leave a job. Consequently, when she asked for this money and didn't get it, she went to see the boss to complain, and was sacked – she claims *before* she swore at him. He claims she swore at him before he sacked her.

(d) Mr Taylor claimed initially that an additional reason for sacking her was her poor attendance record; documents produced in court proved that she had a better record than most male employees at the firm.

Discussion

The Tribunal decided by a 2–1 majority that Ms Krangel's dismissal was not unfair (the one member who thought it was unfair was a woman – the other two were men). On the evidence you have been given and any more you can find (the case was heard in May 1977), what would have been your decision if you had been a member of the Tribunal? You might, before coming to a decision, try to organize a mock trial, with 'Ms Krangel' and 'Mr Taylor' coming before it to answer questions.

Drafting a notice

It could be argued that a building site is no place for women to work, but since the Sex Discrimination Act became law in 1976, any job – with a few necessary exceptions – must be equally open to persons of either sex; it was almost certainly as a result of this Act that Ms Krangel got the job as a bricklayer.

Suppose that you were in charge of a building site on which women are shortly to be employed for the first time; what problems do you think this would create for the men working on the site, and for the women? Discuss the issue in groups of four or five and arrange for someone to report back the findings of your group to the rest of the class.

Then, using your group's discussions and the reports from the other groups as a basis, write a note to be put in the pay packets of all the men working on the site explaining the situation, outlining the difficulties that may arise, asking them to make allowances for the problems that may arise, and suggesting steps they might take to ensure that the women may quickly and smoothly become a normal and accepted part of the working team; and draft a note to be sent to all prospective women employees, warning them of the problems they are likely to face if they do decide to work on the site, and advising them how they may best meet and overcome these problems.

Unit 9

Technical comprehension and technical work

Read the following passage; then answer the questions below.

The aim of the maker of a wooden roof was to brace the timber in such a way that the roof would sit on the building like a lid without trying to spread itself and exert a thrust which would endanger the walls, as only light buttresses, if any, were to be used. In addition, there was danger from high winds. To meet these problems four great roof families were developed:

       tie-beam roofs;
       trussed-rafter roofs;
       arch-braced roofs;
       hammer-beam roofs.

The first is a simple roof that you can see in any cowshed; a beam fastens the foot of one rafter to the foot of its opposite member, making a triangle. This produces an ugly effect with high-pitched roofs, but if they are fastened to each other higher up, so that each couple forms a letter A you have *a trussed-rafter roof*. In practice, they have either two small extra pieces under the cross-bar, or two ties which cross each other like a letter X turned sideways. This type of roof is never carved, but if you make a complete curve of rafters under the cross-piece it forms a 'waggon-ceiling', which may be richly decorated.

This roof imposes a weight on the wall but no thrust, unless the timbers warp. The *arch-braced roof* is virtually a wooden arch connected, if at all, from rafter to rafter by a collar placed high up. It exerts considerable thrust on the walls, and an effort is made to distribute this thrust by carrying a wall post down the face of either wall. The arch-braced roof produced an effect of clear height and it could display some moulding and other carving.

The *hammer-beam roof* was developed from the arch-braced roof. The wall-post was turned into a bracket supporting a hammer-beam, a piece of wood fastened to both the foot of the rafter and to the wall-plate. It projected into the hall or nave and from its end rose another arch-shaped bracket which was fastened to the rafter as it ascended.

                 E. Vale *How to Look at Old Buildings*

(a) From the descriptions given above, and introducing no further information, draw simple diagrams, such as may be used to illustrate the text, of each of the following: a tie-beam roof; a trussed-rafter roof; a waggon-ceiling; an arch-braced roof; a hammer-beam roof. You may find it useful to label your diagrams, but use only the terms used by the author.

(b) The book from which this passage was taken was intended 'particularly for people now living in the country for the first time to help them to use their leisure constructively'. What indications are there in the passage that it was intended for the reader who may have some interest in, but little practical knowledge of building techniques? Do you think the descriptions could have been simpler or clearer? If so, where do you think such a reader would encounter problems, and how could they have been cleared up? (*Note*: you may find that your attempts to draw the roofs from the descriptions given will help you to understand whether such difficulties do exist, and if so, what they are.)

(c) Try to find, in a book intended for construction or architectural students, a description of one of the types of roof described in the passage above. Copy it out. In what ways is it different from the passage above?

(d) Try to find in your own area examples of the types of roof described by the author. How accurately do they conform to his descriptions? Could you recognize them from his descriptions alone?

Technical Material

(a) Below are reproduced three sketches showing the various elements of certain types of roof. They are labelled, but some of the labels have been replaced by letters; the correct labels are listed below, but in random order. Indicate which you think is the correct label for each letter. (*Note*: you may need to use some labels more than once.)

List of terms needed, with some definitions:
Purlin: longitudinal member laid parallel with wall plate and ridge beam some way up slopes of roof;
king-post: upright timber connecting a tie-beam and a collar beam with the ridge beam;
wall-plate: timber laid longitudinally on top of a wall;

wall post; arched-brace;
common rafter; sole plate;
hammer-beam; strut.
ridge;

(b) The following elements of the roof are shown labelled on the sketches; with the definitions above as a guide, write definitions of them, such as might appear in the glossary of a book on building written for the interested layman:
   strut; tie-beam; collar beam; queen-post; brace; corbel.

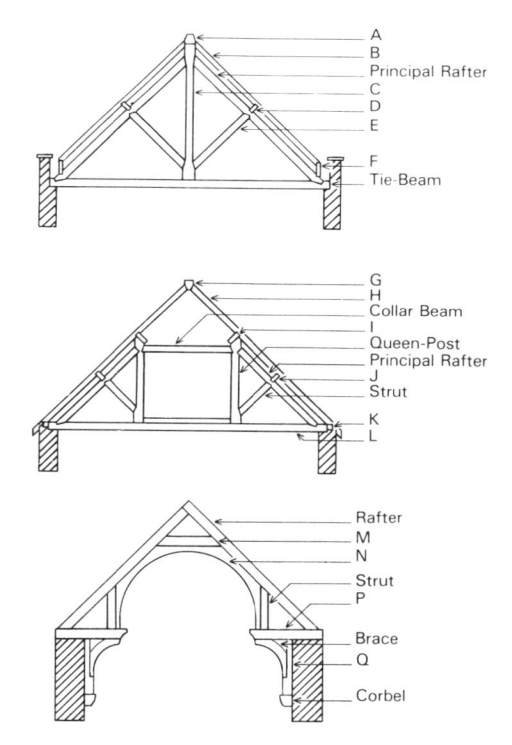

```
A
B
Principal Rafter
C
D
E
F
Tie-Beam

G
H
Collar Beam
I
Queen-Post
Principal Rafter
J
Strut
K
L

Rafter
M
N
Strut
P
Brace
Q
Corbel
```

Diagrams from N. Pevsner *Buildings of England*

Technical Vocabulary

Below is shown a diagram, together with a description, of a modern type of roof truss. Several words in the description have been omitted; these are listed below the description, but in random order.

Copy out the passage, inserting the correct words (*note*: two of the words you will need to use more than once).

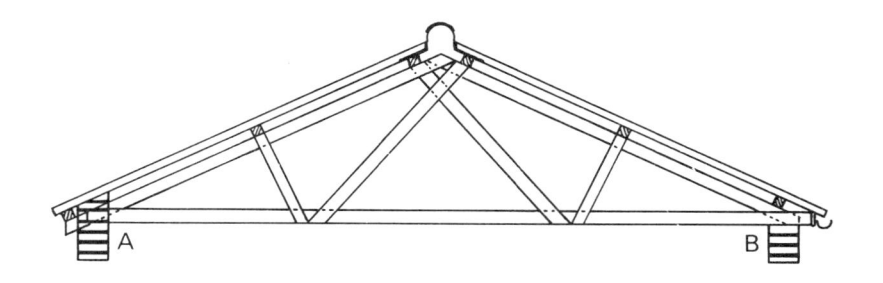

The type of timber roof truss illustrated here, drawn for 16ft. clear —— between 9in. brick walls and carrying asbestos-cement sheets at 25° —— has several interesting features.

At the —— the rafter and the —— running nearly parallel with it are in the same —— so that both those from the left-hand side of the drawing are on top (when marking) of those two from the right. This gives only two thicknesses, as it were, at each —— so that only two members have to be lined up before nailing or bolting together. If nailing is adopted, as it would normally be for short spans, there is little difficulty in —— them.

Further, the members lie flatter than in many other arrangements, except for double rafters and —— (which certainly build up a substantial thickness) and there is thus less twisting and —— —— in the members.

Even more useful, from a practical aspect, are the large areas in contact at the joints. Near the ——, for instance, there are four joints, into any of which, using 4in. by 2in. timber, it would be easy to drive four nails at reasonable spacing. There is none of the dangerous skimpiness of trying to joint 2in. of a —— —— to one —— end, and the other 2in. of the 4in. width to the end of the other ——.

The —— details shown at A and B are alternative arrangements for farm buildings, A being for —— —— and B for ——. Wall plates are often omitted in such work, the trusses being clipped and bolted down several feet into the walls.

The Illustrated Carpenter and Builder

List of words to be used:

Tie-beams	stresses	apex	eaves
plane	ridge	rafter	intersection
bricked-up	open	brace	clinching
king-post	secondary	pitch	span

Unit 10

Comprehension

Read the following passage, and then consider the questions raised after it.

What can the householder rely on if he and the builder fall out?

First, you will have been wise to have had the builder or installer agree to independent arbitration being brought into play eventually, if you find yourself at odds. He may nominate his professional association or institute, or you may between you settle for the Institute of Arbitrators.

What *can* go wrong between you and the builder, or his workman? 'The most common kind of complaint is "The work isn't done properly",' the legal expert says. 'The down-the-line guidance on that is, "If you can show that the work hasn't been carried out as it should be you needn't pay for it."' But there may be complications.

There may be an exclusion clause in the estimate or contract exempting faults in goods supplied by sub-contractors, for example. Also, to 'show' that a bodge has been done doesn't mean advancing your own opinion to that effect, or quoting a brother-in-law in the council's works department. It would probably mean calling in another builder for an opinion or a surveyor.

Something else that crops up is a job not being finished by an agreed date. The law is simple on this: if nothing is mentioned about a completion date it's understood that the work must be finished within a reasonable time, not be dragged on inordinately.

A worry for many people from the outset of a job is what would happen if the builder should exceed his estimate. The plain fact is that the builder is bound by his quoted price, and can only increase it on account of extras asked for or agreed by you.

If the job goes ahead with no price having been agreed on, and if the final bill seems really inordinate and the householder decides to take a stand he may well be on good ground. The builder may only charge what any other reasonable firm in the same line of business would charge for the same job.

It may seem only a detail, but clearing-away is an important part of a household repair operation, and the original agreement should state that the builder will take away his materials, tools and rubbish within, say, 14 days of finishing the job. By the same token, it should be agreed that materials ordered-up for the work, not used and taken away by him, should be credited to the householder in the final bill. Beyond that, what about the valuable lead piping ripped out when the new central heating is installed? Or the ornate marble fireplace removed with the clearing away of a chimney breast? The agreement should stipulate that these be left for the householder, or that he be given a credit for them.

(a) What can go wrong between a builder and a householder?
(b) What should a householder do in order to get the best conditions and service from a builder?
(c) What legal obligations are there on a builder once he has taken on a job for a householder?

Letter writing

Personal letters, to friends and relatives

In these you can write freely of things which are of joint interest and concern, at any length. Your style of writing and the words you use can be whatever you wish, though you should show some interest in the person to whom you are sending the letter and you should choose the material to interest him.

Personal letters are usually laid out with your address and the date in the top right-hand corner. The greeting (e.g. 'Dear John') and the farewell (e.g. 'Yours ever') should be suitable, though they are very varied and often amusing.

Here is an example of a personal letter.

```
                                        5, Woodlands,
                                            Hove,
                                              Sussex,
                                                BN5 8QT
                            7th December 1979

Dear Maud and Reg,

    It doesn't seem fair that I should be working hard while you
two are on holiday, and in Walsall of all places! I hope you
are having a good time there, with lots to eat and drink, so that
you are both in good shape for work when you get back home.

    We are all OK, despite the miserable weather, and we send our
love.
                        Yours,
                        Brian and Co.
P.S.  Lisa still has Antony's rucksack.  Sorry!
```

Business letters

If your communication is to be carried out properly, then you must make sure that you give all the information the person to whom your are writing requires.

For this reason, certain ways of setting out a business letter have become set, and you should follow them.

You should give your own address, usually at the top right-hand corner of the page; the address of the person or firm you are writing to, usually below your own address, but on the left-hand side of the page; and the date, usually directly below your address. It should appear like this:

```
                              184, Mount Ararat Road,
                                  Putney,
                                      London,
                                          SW15 2BF
                    28th June 1979
Messrs. R.S. Scott and Co.,
12, Hill Brow,
London,
N11 3ZZ

Dear Sirs,
    I wish to be considered for the post of .....
```

Note the punctuation throughout and the capital letter for 'Sirs'. The commas in the addresses are optional nowadays and are often left out.

Your writing should be neat and clear preferably on white, unlined paper. The letter should be to the point and as short as possible. It must contain all the necessary information, however, and include essential extra documents, such as testimonials.

The letter may be ended in one of two ways: (i) 'Yours faithfully' or 'Yours truly' if you are writing to someone you do not know. If you begin a business letter with 'Dear Sir (Sirs)' you will end with 'Your faithfully'; (ii) 'Yours sincerely', if you are writing to someone you have met or whom you know well enough to address by name. A business letter beginning 'Dear Mr. Scott' will end with 'Yours sincerely'.

Note that in these endings, the first word always has a capital letter and the second word never. The farewell phrase usually appears on the right of the page and is completed by a comma with the writer's name on the next line below.

Never add a postscript.

The envelope should be addressed as below, though the commas may be left out:

                    Messrs. R.S. Scott and Co.,
                          12, Hill Brow,
                             London,
                              N11 3ZZ

Note that if you use 'Esq.' (i.e. esquire) after a name, you do not use 'Mr.' before it. Thus either 'Mr. R. Webber' or 'R. Webber, Esq.' is correct.

Here is an example of a business letter:

                              184, Mount Ararat Road,
                                   Putney,
                                   London,
                                        SW15 2BF
                          28th June 1979

    Messrs. R.S. Scott and Co.,
    12, Hill Brow,
    London,
    N11 3ZZ

    Dear Sirs,
        I wish to be considered for the post of yard sub-manager with your firm.
        I am twenty-two years of age, unmarried and live conveniently near to your premises. I enjoy good health and have no history of lateness with my present company.
        I have two 'O' Levels and four CSE's (certificates enclosed) and since leaving York Road Comprehensive School in 1973 I have risen in my present firm from labourer-clerk to assistant materials controller (see enclosed testimonial).
        I live with my parents, play rugby for my school's 'Old Boys' team and take an interest in weight-lifting. I also attend evening classes in English, Mathematics and Building at Richmond College of Further Education.
                          Yours faithfully,

                          Raymond Webber

(a) Write letters from an imaginary householder to a builder:
   (i) asking him to install a new fireplace.
   (ii) asking him to install central heating.
   (iii) complaining of overpricing in the bill.
   (iv) complaining of poor workmanship in altering the fireplace.
   (v) asking him to remove the tools and rubbish he has left behind.

(b) Write the letters in reply to each of the above from the builder.
(c) Write a letter of application for a job you would like in the building industry.
(d) Write testimonials:
    (i) for yourself
    (ii) for someone you know well.
(e) Write letters on each of the following subjects:
    (i) asking for details of membership of the local sports club.
    (ii) asking for details about the Duke of Edinburgh's Award scheme.
    (iii) from someone signed 'Anxious' to a magazine asking for advice about a friend.
    (iv) from someone signed 'Disgusted' to a local paper complaining about local teenagers.
    (v) to a Bank Manager asking about opening an account.
    (vi) to the BBC asking for free tickets to a television show you like.
    (vii) to your local town hall complaining about bus services.
    (viii) to a friend in a building firm asking for materials and advice on their use.
    (ix) to a local travel agents asking for brochures about Spain.
    (x) to a guest-house booking a holiday.
    (xi) to someone you met on holiday and would like to meet again.
    (xii) to a brother, sister or friend who is living away from home.
    (xiii) to your old head teacher, who has asked you to come back to school to talk about your present job, accepting or refusing the invitation.
    (xiv) to a neighbour complaining about their noise.
    (xv) to someone who is ill in hospital.
    (xvi) to offer sympathy to someone who has suffered a close bereavement.

Unit 11

Comprehension (including research and organization of material)

Read the following passage; then answer the questions below.

One significant result of the Industrial Revolution in building must be that natural materials of varied (or heterogeneous) composition will be replaced by artificial materials. Because these artificial materials can be tested in a laboratory their composition will be fixed (or homogeneous).

For one thing, the laws of Economics will demand the use of such artificial materials. Steel girders and reinforced concrete are two examples of materials which builders and architects can use with almost total confidence, since their capabilities and potentialities can be calculated with almost total accuracy, whereas in the old wooden beam there may be lurking some treacherous knot, and the very way in which it is squared up means a very heavy loss in material.

In certain fields, the technical experts have already spoken. Water supplies and lighting services are rapidly being evolved; central heating has begun to take into consideration the structure of walls and windows – that is to say, surfaces that are likely to cool and therefore reduce its effectiveness – and in consequence traditional stone walls, sometimes up to three feet thick, are being replaced by the more efficient and more economical cavity walls in breeze slabs. Features of buildings which for centuries remained unquestioned are now found to be less useful and less attractive than we had assumed; roofs which no longer need to be pointed for the purpose of throwing off water; the enormous and handsome window embrasures which now annoy us, since they imprison the light and deprive us of it; the massive timbers, as thick as you please and heavy for all eternity, but which will spring and split if placed near a radiator, while a patent board $\frac{1}{8}$ inch thick will remain intact.

Le Corbusier *Towards a New Architecture* (translated by Etchells (adapted))

(a) Usually the phrase 'Industrial Revolution' refers to the period roughly between 1770 and 1840 during which England and the rest of Europe became industrial societies;

in this passage, however, the author is using the phrase in quite a different sense. What does he mean by the term? How would he expect the reader to know that he was using the term not in its normal sense?
(b) Look up in a dictionary the meanings of the words 'homogeneous' and 'heterogeneous' then explain what the author means by homogeneous composition and heterogeneous composition.
(c) (i) Make a list, as far as possible in your own words, of all the advantages mentioned in the passage of using artificial building materials.
 (ii) Make a list of any disadvantages you can think of, or that you can collect from other sources, of using artificial building materials.
 (iii) Suppose you heard an argument between two people claiming that in general artificial building materials were to be preferred to traditional materials, and the other disputing this, both making use of the material in questions (c)(i) and (ii) above; which side would you support, and why?

Research

(a) By making use of as many sources as possible (including, perhaps, someone in authority in a building firm), make a list of materials used in building today which were not in use 100 years ago.
(b) Using one sentence for each, write a definition such as could be understood by someone just starting a TEC Construction course, of the materials you have listed in (a) above.
(c) State for each what material(s) it has replaced.

Letter writing

Suppose a client of the firm for which you work has written to ask for some repair work to be done to his house, but stresses that he wants it done 'in good traditional material, none of your modern plastic trash'. Having inspected the work to be done, you decide that while traditional material could be used, it would be cheaper, more efficient, and just as aesthetically satisfying if a more modern material were used. (*Note*: look up the word 'aesthetically' in a dictionary if you don't know what it means.) Draft a letter for the manager of the firm to sign explaining the situation.

You should remember that, as the client is paying for the work, he has a right to have the work carried out as he specifies. Your letter should make it clear that you are not laying down conditions, that you will use the material he specifies if he insists, but point out all the advantages of not doing so in the particular circumstances (that is, write only about his house, don't talk in general terms about the advantages of modern materials over traditional ones).

Vocabulary

Prefixes

In question (b) in the Comprehension section, you were asked to use a dictionary to find the meanings of 'homogeneous' and 'heterogeneous'; you may have noticed that the dictionary told you that 'homo-' means 'the same' and that 'hetero-' means 'different'; these parts of words are called **prefixes** and they add to or change the meaning of that part of the word which follows. If we know what prefixes mean we can often work out the meaning of a word that is unfamiliar to us.

In the grid opposite, some common prefixes with their meanings are in the column on the left; along the top are some Latin words with their meanings. Copy out the grid, then fill in as many spaces as you can by combining prefixes with Latin words in the spaces where they meet (a few are done for you, to show you the idea). Try first to use your own knowledge of language to fill in as many spaces as you can, then use a dictionary to fill in the others that you didn't know, or couldn't think of. (*Note*: it will not be possible to find words to fill all the spaces.)

	dico dict (say)	scribo script (write)	pono ponere (place)	jacere ject (throw)	traho tract (draw)	latere (carry)	porto (carry)	duco duct (lead)	grado gress (walk)	cedo cess (go)
re (again)										
pre (before)	predict									
sub (under)										
con contra (against)										
post (after)			postpone							
pro (forward)				project						
trans (through across)										
e, ex (out)										
in, im (in)										

Unit 12

Note-taking

No doubt you have already, on the TEC course, been asked to 'take notes' – and such notes have probably taken various forms; often, perhaps, they will have been dictated word for word; sometimes, on the other hand, you may have just jotted down an odd word to jog your memory about something you already know. But at times you will need to take fairly full notes, perhaps from a book, perhaps while listening to a lecturer, which will enable you later to recall quickly important information in some detail. Copying passages from a book is no use – it takes too long, and you may as well re-read the book, rather than your notes; on the other hand, unconnected scraps of information will be almost useless. You must be able to see the connections between the facts you are reading or the information you pick up is probably valueless.

(a) The following is a set of notes made by a student from a book on central heating. He has tried to organize his material so that it falls into clearly defined but related sections. You may like to discuss as a class how effective you think these notes are and how, perhaps, they could be improved. Do they make sense to you? Can you rewrite the original passage (not in the author's words, obviously, but sufficiently closely to convey his 'message' in detail and without distortion)? Try to do so, then compare your version with the author's (you can find a copy of his book in most libraries); if you find your version is inaccurate or incomplete, try to decide whether this is your fault or the fault of the person who produced the notes.

HEATING SYSTEMS: HOT WATER

Traditional systems.
Small solid boiler connected to hot water tank and radiators.
Water circulates ∴ different temps. in different parts of the system (convention); called *'Gravity system'*.
Such systems known as *'direct systems'* – water in radiators from same source as water in taps.

Disadvantages:
(i) all parts of system must be corrosion-resistant.
(ii) heating system goes cold if water is drawn off for bath, etc.

Indirect systems
Water system incorporates inner coil ('heat exchanger') – this heats domestic water 'indirectly'; boiler and radiator have separate systems.
Header tank is usually necessary:
(i) to provide initial filling of heating system;
(ii) to allow for expansion and contraction of water.
H.T. must be situated above highest part of system.

In *automatic feed cylinder systems*: no H.T. needed.
Special heat exchanger allows water to feed from cold storage to heating system BUT
When heating circuit full, air bubble forms to separate systems:
When water expands, air bubble displaced; returns to original position when heating switched off and water contracts.

(b) Below is an extract from the same book; in fact, this passage follows immediately that on which the notes in question (a) are based. Using the notes in question (a) as a model (in your own version, if you think you have improved them), draft a set of notes on the material in these two paragraphs. Later in the year you may be set a test in which you will be expected to answer questions on the material, using your notes only.

There are some boilers that incorporate a hot water tank, or calorifier, as an integral piece of equipment. This type of appliance is called a combination boiler, and is more widely used on the Continent than in England. Oil- and gas-fired combination boilers are available and, while they are larger than conventional boilers of similar output, the hot water storage capacity is usually less than that which would be required, because the calorifier, being near to the heat source, provides for a very quick hot water recovery.

With the development of the small domestic pump or accelerator it was possible to dispense with large bore pipes previously necessary with gravity systems, and this, coupled with the introduction of copper and other thin-walled tubing, gave rise to the advent of the 'small bore' system. With pumped circulation round the system it is, of course, possible, to achieve more flexibility in pipe runs, since any possible effects of natural convection can largely be disregarded. It is, however, fairly common practice to provide a separate gravity circuit from the boiler to the hot water cylinder and thus only use the pump for the heating circuit. In fact, this is quite an important feature of systems using solid fuel or natural draught oil boilers, where the hot water tank is used to dissipate the heat output which exists even at 'low fire'. It also facilitates separate control of the heating system simply by switching the pump on and off as required. This arrangement does, however, impose restrictions on the layout of the system, since the hot water cylinder must be located above the level of the boiler and fairly near to it. In addition, the recovery rate of hot water is totally dependent on the rate of gravity circulation between the boiler and the cylinder. In consequence, it is sometimes advantageous to incorporate the hot water cylinder on the pumped circuit from the boiler. This provides greater freedom in positioning the cylinder and also results in quicker hot water recovery.

B. J. King and J. E. Beer *Home Heating*

Technical vocabulary and description

(a) Below are diagrams showing the differences between direct and indirect systems of central heating, but with all the original labelling omitted. Copy the diagrams and add sufficient labelling to indicate how each system works. Then write a short paragraph, referring to the diagrams, explaining the differences between the two systems.

DIRECT SYSTEM   INDIRECT SYSTEM

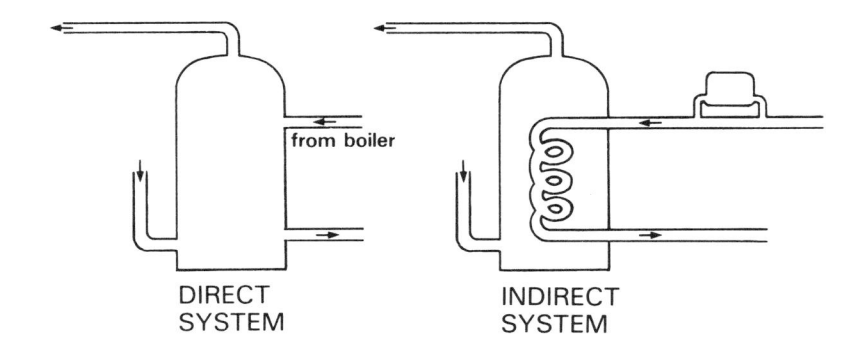

Diagrams from R. Warring *All About Home Heating*

Unit 13

Discussion (including critical work); personal writing

Read the following passage; then answer the questions below.

It all began with the floor of the lounge. Nasty, it was. Broken, cracked, rotten, and with as much bounce as a trampoline. A fitted carpet was the answer, but we already had a perfectly good unfitted carpet. A quick phone round the wood merchants proved that a completely new pine floor would cost £50 if I laid it myself. There is nothing easier than ripping out a wood floor. Out it comes, and you fling the boards through the open window. I missed. Twice. At 12.30 on a freezing December night, with the new floor lying in the street and the rubble of the old in the front garden, my wife and I were standing outside puttying in new windows. At 1.30 I was carrying in the new boards to lay them up the stairs, which was the only place they would fit. At ten the next morning I was carrying the whole lot back outside again, since there wasn't room to work the saw in the hall. Two days later the job was done; so I tackled the bathroom, the loo, the kitchen.

The dining room was my *coup de grâce*. From the tiled, papered, cupboard-fitted, mixer-laden, air-conditioned kitchen you enter a room which retains the true original aura of the Gardner residence. Wires dangle from the wall, waiting for lights. Walls shower the unwary with clouds of dried plaster awaiting repairs. (Did you know that a bag of Blue Hawk patching powder costs about one-third of those proprietary fillers?) Floorboards lie uneasily to trap the unwary. It's my before-and-after room, and it may well stay that way.

Adapted from *The Guardian*

(a) This description is an example of someone creating humour from a situation which, at the time it occurred must have been annoying, frustrating, even embarrassing. What means does the writer adopt to create humour from the situation? If you find this a difficult question to answer study the following passage, which attempts to narrate what the author is describing in one part of the passage but with all the humour excluded; try to suggest what is lacking in this description. Secondly, try to rewrite the rest of the passage in the same vein, again excluding all trace of humour, and note carefully what you find it necessary to change, because in the original it strikes you as funny.

> The floor of our lounge was cracked and rotten and badly needed repairing. (The alternative was to replace our perfectly good carpet with a new, fitted carpet, but we did not see the point of that.) I discovered that if I laid it myself I could have a new pine floor for £50. So I removed the old floorboards, but in throwing them outside, two windows were broken. Before we could bring in the new floorboards we had to repair the panes, and by now it was late at night and very cold.

(b) What suggestions are there in the original passage that the writer is (i) not wholly incompetent at performing practical tasks, and (ii) less efficient than he thought himself to be?
(c) One way of coping with disturbing or embarrassing memories is to turn them into jokes against ourselves, as the writer of this passage is probably trying to do. Try to narrate something that happened to you that at the time was certainly not funny in such a way that it will amuse other people and perhaps yourself.

Verse study

> I brought a 'Death of Nelson' home, where I
> Hung it, by inadvertence, on a fly.
>   Down crashed the heavy frame, off the fly flew
> And how my curses rang! Frankly, I own
> To a sad lack of humour when alone –
> Like you, by God, and you, and even you!
>
> Robert Graves

(a) What point is Robert Graves making in this short poem?
(b) What similarities or differences do you see between Graves' attitude and the attitude of the writer in the passage in the Discussion section above?

Technical description

Suppose that you have been asked to write for a Do-It-Yourself magazine an article describing for a layman how he could do a basically simple task with which you are familiar. You should choose a job that *is* basically simple for someone with experience, but one for which a builder is normally called since it involves comparatively simple but technical expertise. You should bear in mind the following points:

(a) tell him what tools he will need – and be precise; it's no use saying he will need a file if it *has* to be a rat-tail file;
(b) tell him what materials he will need – and again, be precise; include where relevant the quantities, sizes, exact types of wood, cement and so on, and other important details;
(c) consider whether you should try to avoid using the word 'you' – try to remember the conclusions you came to when you discussed the matter in the Comprehension exercise of Unit 3 (question (d) on passage B);
(d) consider whether a diagram or diagrams would help; but if you do use a diagram, draw it large, keep it simple, do not put in any irrelevant details, label it carefully, and refer to it in the text (you may find it useful to look again at the diagrams in Unit 12);
(e) write the instructions in a list (perhaps like this list of instructions) as a set of numbered points, not as a paragraph;
(f) make sure that you get the sequence of activities exactly right;
(g) write in short sentences with only one instruction, however simple, in each sentence;
(h) assume that the person you are writing for knows nothing about the job;
(i) warn him of all possible mistakes and pitfalls that you can think of;
(j) tell him how he can test whether the job has been successfully completed;
(k) finally, check what you have written, and make sure that you have followed all these instructions; if you have not, ask yourself if there is a good reason.

When you have completed it in rough, hand it to an appropriate technical lecturer and ask him for his comments on the accuracy of what you have written, then rewrite it, taking note of his comments, before handing it to your communications lecturer for his comments on how it might be improved in grammar, spelling, style, presentation and so on. Finally, bearing his comments in mind, rewrite it yet again.

This will probably seem to you a lot of boring and unnecessary work, but you should remember that few people, even fully experienced writers, can ever write anything sufficiently good for circulation without its going through several drafts, since every draft will show improvements (the authors of this book wrote each chapter several times).

Use of hyphens

In the sentence 'If you want anything doing, do it yourself' the words 'do it yourself' are written, naturally, as three separate words. Yet in the preceding exercise you were asked to write an article for a 'Do-It-Yourself magazine' where the same words are pulled together by hyphens. The reason is that here the words have been pulled together to tell us one thing – and only one thing – about the magazine, in just the same way as the words 'Carpentry' or 'Music' tell us only one thing about each of the magazines in the titles 'Carpentry Monthly' or 'Music Magazine'; several other examples can be found in the passage at the beginning of this Unit.

Where two or more words are used to describe something or someone, but tell us quite different things about him, or it, no hyphen is required – for example, 'a strong, healthy man' is *both* strong *and* healthy – the qualities may be allied, but they are not the same; similarly, 'a long, boring book' is both long and boring, but you would need a hyphen in 'long-lost brother' – he is not long *and* lost. Write out the following phrases and sentences inserting hyphens where you think they are necessary. But don't assume that you will need to put hyphens in every example.

    A used car salesman required.
    The most up to date methods of motorway construction.
    The firm were told to bring its accounts up to date.
    A morning after the night before feeling.
    In the nineteenth century houses were built largely for speculation.
    Many eighteenth century houses are still in habitable condition.
    The water cement ratio should not exceed 0.4 in HAC.
    extra sensory perception.
    a hit and run driver.
    solve the problem by algebra, not by trial and error methods.
    he found the right solution, but only by trial and error.

The electrically heated storage system and the gas heated instantaneous systems, both with simple draw offs, are easily installed.

For sale: seven transistor radio sets (*note*: there are two possible answers to this one; explain how they are different in meaning).

Now go back through previous exercises and check whether you omitted any hyphens which should have been inserted.

Unit 14

Discussion (including comprehension and organization material)

Some years ago Joan Littlewood developed the idea of the 'Fun Palace'. It was to be established in a park in east London and its aim was to counteract boredom; she felt that large numbers of the population were bored for a lot of the time. Part of a publicity handout advertising this 'Fun Palace' is reproduced below, and questions (a) to (e) are based on it.

Joan Littlewood presents the FIRST GIANT SPACE MOBILE IN THE WORLD

it moves in light turns winter into summer... toy... EVERYBODY'S what is it?

Joan Littlewood, with architects, designers, engineers, cyberneticians, cooks, topologists, toy-makers, flow-masters, think clowns, offers you the occasion to enjoy, 24 hours a day, space, light, movement, air, sun, water, in a new dimension.

for your delight

Juke Box Information	Observation Decks
Adult Toys	Nurseries
Star Gazing	Music
Science Gadgetry	Theatre Clownery
News Service	Instant Camera
Tele-communication	Fireworks
Swank Promenades	Recording Sessions
Hide Aways	Kunst Dabbling
Dance Floors	Gala Days & Nights
Drink	Genius Chat
Rallies	Gossip Revues
Battles of Flowers	Laboratories
Concerts	Food
Learning Machines	Ateliers

(a) Are the items listed in an organized way? If so, what is the basis of that organization? If you think that they are set down at random, do you think that this is due to carelessness, or might there be a good psychological reason for it?
(b) What type of people do you think Joan Littlewood is hoping to attract into the Fun Palace? What evidence is there for your answer?
(c) (i) Rearrange all the items in the list into three columns. In column A place all the items which are known to you; in column B place all the items which you are not certain about, but which you think you understand; in column C place all the items which are meaningless to you.
 (ii) Compare the lists you have drawn up. The lecturer could list on the board all items that all members of the class have placed in column A; it can then be assumed that these present no problem. If, however, you have placed in column A any item which does not appear on the list on the board, try to define this item so that all members of the class understand exactly what you think it is. Now the lecturer can list on the board all the items which every member of the class has placed in column B; again, if you have listed in this column any item which other members of the class have placed in column C, try to define this item in such a way that other members of the class understand exactly what you think it is. If, for any of the items which you have now defined, there is a significant difference in meaning between your definition and the definitions offered by other members of the class, try to account for the disagreement. Is it that one of you is at fault, or does the disagreement arise because the leaflet is not clear enough? If the class decides that it is impossible to tell, from the leaflet, which of the differing definitions is the accurate one for any particular item, discuss whether this is due to carelessness on the part of the leaflet writer, or whether it could be deliberate. If you think it might be deliberate, can you suggest why the writer might *want* to leave something unclear?
 (iii) For the items discussed in (c)(ii) how could you discover which of the definitions, if any, were near to the intentions of the writer of the leaflet? Or, where no definitions were offered, how could you find out what the items were?

Practical work

(a) Suppose you were asked to join a committee formed to organize a fun palace in your town or area. Make a list of the activities which you think should be included (you may include or exclude any items from the list in the leaflet, but you should add some items of your own). Next, make a list of all the categories of people you would want to attract to the fun palace; you might, for instance, want to include, among other categories: children, teenagers, old age pensioners; men and women; manual workers and white collar workers − complete the list so that it contains as wide a spread of the population as possible (some of the categories will, of course, overlap).

(b) Now draw a grid showing your activities in a column on the left, and your categories of people horizontally along the top. The beginnings of one such grid are shown below. In each square put a tick if you think that the item would, in general, interest the category of person with which it intersects (in the example below, it is expected that the jukebox would interest children, teenagers, but not parents; stargazing would interest all three; pop concerts, it is assumed, would be of interest only to teenagers). In your table, unless each category of person has a substantial number of ticks beneath it, it is not being adequately provided for, and you should add further activities to cater for them. Similarly, reading across, if any of your items have very few ticks, it implies that their appeal is limited, and you might consider omitting them.

	Children	Teenagers	Parents
Jukebox	✓	✓	
Stargazing	✓	✓	✓
Pop Concerts		✓	

(c) Having completed your table to your own satisfaction, preferably having discussed it with some other members of the class and amended it as a result, suppose that your suggestions are accepted by the Committee and the Fun Palace is to open in a few weeks' time. Draft a publicity leaflet, designed for wide circulation, aimed to appeal to as wide a range of the population of your area as possible.

or

Working in pairs, prepare and record short interviews for a local radio station immediately prior to the opening of the Fun Palace. One member of each pair should act as a radio station interviewer, asking leading questions, the other member using the interview to gain publicity for the Fun Palace. (*Note*: the interviewer should not be aggressive; he should try to organize his questions so that they will give the person being interviewed opportunity to gain useful publicity for the project.)

Research and letter writing

Look at the activities you listed in answering question (a) in the Practical Work section above. If your list is at all lengthy it is almost certain that there are some activities in it which are not catered for in the district where you live.

(a) Find out the nearest town or district which provides for one such activity (don't choose one that could not possibly be catered for – for example, you cannot provide for mountaineering if you live in East Anglia). Using any means you can think of, find out how long it would take you to get there, what the fare would be (or the cost of petrol if you have your own transport), what time you would have to leave to get home at night, and any other details you would require to know if you were going to use these facilities.

(b) Find out which official on your Council is responsible for organizing leisure activity provision.

(c) Write a letter to this official requesting the Council to consider providing for the amenity or activity you investigated in (a). Use the information you have collected in that section to strengthen your case where it will do so. If two or more members of the class can agree on an activity, draft the letter jointly and send it out with more than one signature. This will make your case stronger.

Unit 15

Comprehension (including critical work)

Read the following passage; then answer the questions below.

The division between those who live in council houses and those who do not is essentially and deeply unhappy. This is a deep division, for one-third of the population live in publicly provided housing. I think it is a division that in a number of subtle ways poisons the social life of the country, it splits us into two, each part having different outlooks, different standards, different loyalties, even different approaches to life. If we are concerned (as surely we must be) to level out the differences in our class structure, then this obnoxious division in housing must be got rid of. I suppose the situation we should aim for is one where, in addition to there being a great variety of dwelling types available, there would also be a variety of types of tenure, from which people could make a choice, and where they could move easily from one type to another as they desired, and not as some system of housing provision dictated.

The trouble with so much of our housing development is that it tends to be so rigid and uniform. What people seem to like is to have a great variety of accommodation to choose from; they seem to like large houses, small houses, large flats, small flats, some with gardens, some without, but all more or less jumbled together with every place different. Then they can have the pleasure of ferreting out a place that suits them, they can express their personalities through their dwellings when they are like this much more easily and effectively than when the choice is between one semi and another, identical, one. As I travel about the country and look at what is happening in what I might call loosely the emerging middle classes, I am struck by the enormous source of interest that seems to be provided for these people by their homes. Again, when travelling by train I look at the rows of fairly poor houses backing on to the railway lines – you know the kind I mean for there are millions of them still – terraced houses with back additions and little strips of gardens – but I see bits tacked on, I see flowers in the gardens, little patches of mown grass, pigeon lofts, and, of course, sheds; and I feel that those houses, miserable though they may be in many respects, nevertheless provide a creative outlet for the occupants in a way that a flat in a tower block, where you can't drive a nail into a wall without permission, does not and cannot achieve. If I had to pin to one single piece of advice to planners of housing estates, I think I would say, 'Don't forget the sheds'.

C. Buchanan *The State of Britain*

(a) What does the author hope to gain by the use of the word 'essentially' in the first sentence?

(b) (i) When the author refers to divisions between council house dwellers and those who own their houses, what precise divisions do you think he has in mind? You might try to answer the questions by discussing and suggesting examples of the different outlooks, standards, loyalties and approaches to life he refers to later in the paragraph.

 (ii) Why does the author see the division as a division in our class structure? What assumptions about 'class' lie behind this comment by the author? Would you agree that this is a class division? Explain why.

 (iii) In the second paragraph the author refers to 'What I might loosely call the emerging middle classes'. From what are they emerging? And in what ways might they be becoming middle class? Do you see any conflict between this description of a group of people and the author's desire in the first paragraph to 'level out the differences in class structure'?

(c) What do you think the author has in mind when he refers to so much of our housing development being 'rigid and uniform'?

(d) Do you see any underlying suggestion in the use of the word 'semi' in the phrase 'between one semi and another'? Would the sentence have had the same effect if he had written 'between one semi-detached house and another'?

(e) Why does the author think sheds are so important? Do you agree with him, or do you think he exaggerates their importance, at least in the last sentence?

(f) In the first paragraph the author states that the division into council housing and private housing 'poisons the social life of the country', producing different outlooks and so on; yet in the second paragraph he argues for a variety of housing. Do you see this as a contradiction? Explain why you think it is or is not.

Practical work

The author of the passage quoted in question 1 suggests that there are class divisions between council house tenants and house owners (or house buyers). Certainly it is often suggested in the press and other media that people ought, whenever possible, to buy their own houses, and that there is something inferior about living in a council house; often, indeed, it is suggested (though never stated openly) that council tenants are in some way fraudulent. Before you accept or reject such attitudes, try to find answers to the following questions:

(a) How much does the average council house tenant in your area pay each week in rent?
(b) Do you dislike people you know who live in council houses?
(c) In what ways, if any, does owning one's own house improve someone's character?
(d) How much does a man with a wife and two young children, earning £4,000 a year, and paying off a mortgage at the rate of £12 a week, regain in income tax relief?
(e) Would you feel inferior if you lived in a council house, and if so, in what ways, compared to someone living in a house which he – or his father – owned or was buying? **or** if you do live in a council house, do you feel you would be a better person if you or your family were buying your own house, and if so, in what ways?
(f) How many council house tenants do you know *personally* who run expensive cars or have expensive holidays?
(g) How many cases do you know of *personally*, of people living in their own homes who cannot afford cars or expensive holidays?
(h) Who, throughout his life, pays more for housing – the average council tenant or the average house buyer?

Some of these questions you may find you cannot answer, and for different questions there may be different reasons why you cannot do so. Where you cannot supply an answer try to explain why. Is it simply that the information is not available, or is there quite a different reason?

Do you think it necessary to answer most, at least, of these questions before deciding whether there is any great merit in buying one's own house? If not, which are irrelevant to the issue, and why? And if the answers to the above questions are not easy to find, how do the mass media manage to convey the impression that council house tenants are less worthy of esteem than house buyers? Try to find examples in the press of news items that do convey such suggestions, note what sort of evidence they provide, then check whether that evidence answers any of the questions above; if it doesn't, try to formulate the questions that it does answer.

Lecturette

Suppose you had sufficient money to design a modest house for you and your family to live in. Draw plans of the house you would design, and be prepared to talk to the rest of the class, briefly explaining the plans and explaining what you consider the particular merits of the house. Be prepared to answer from the class questions about your design, and also to answer specific questions about methods of construction. (You may find it useful to specify what sort of area you have in mind for the house – a house in the country will need quite different qualities from a house in the middle of a busy town.)
or
Suppose you had just bought the house you at present live in. What structural and decorative alterations would you make to transform it, as far as possible, into what would be the ideal house *for you*? Draw plans showing the house as it is now, and indicating how you would alter it (assume you have planning permission for all the alterations you wish to make). Be prepared to talk to the rest of the class explaining the nature of the alterations, the reasons for them, and some of the constructional problems and techniques involved. Again, be prepared to answer questions.

Writing an advertisement

Normally, we assume we use words to convey our knowledge and opinions to others as precisely as possible. Sometimes, however, words may be used – without directly lying – to conceal the truth, to mislead our audience. And while most house agents are simply informative in their advertisements, there is no doubt that some are more concerned to mislead. A house described as 'compact' for instance, may simply mean that it is small; a 'patio' sounds elegant and sophisticated, but may prove to be no more than a tiny back yard; 'of unusual design' sounds elegant – it could mean merely that it's a mess.

Try to find local examples of house advertisements which you think *might* be misleading in this way and bring them to class – together with your translations.

Write a house agent's description of your house, making it sound as attractive as possible.

Vocabulary

The use of such words and phrases to cover up something unpleasant is called a 'euphemism'. People will often say 'She passed away' rather than use the more stark 'She died'. Local politicians unwilling to admit that there are slums in their boroughs will refer to 'Grade 3 housing'.

Can you think of euphemisms for:
    he's in jail;
    she stinks (in its literal sense);
    he's drunk;
    living in poverty;
    unemployed (often used by actors)?

Try to collect euphemisms for other activities or states or things that are, or are often thought to be, unpleasant, and in each case try to suggest why the more direct word is often avoided. (Consider that we may sometimes use euphemisms to hide the real aspect of things from ourselves, as well as from other people.)

Unit 16

The Summary (1)

People tend to be repetitive and long-winded, in writing as well as in speaking, when what they want to say could be expressed more simply. A report which was almost as long as the original material would be of little value. Those receiving it might as well read through all the papers and correspondence for themselves.

The value of shortening can be summed up under three heads:
(a) It saves the time of busy people who need to get the main facts as quickly as possible.
(b) It removes the faults of poor expression and the irrelevant matters which have been introduced.
(c) It makes a clear statement of the issue and encourages clear thinking, often as useful to the writer of the report as to those who receive it.

So, we must give some time to studying the techniques of shortening. The process is given different names: *an abstract, precis* or *summary*. The word *summary* is the most convenient to use for our present purpose. How is it to be done? Obviously not just by leaving things out at random. To carry the point to absurd lengths, if every second word in a passage is omitted, the passage will be reduced to half its original length. However, the result will not be a fair report and will not even make sense. To leave out whole sections might produce something more readable, but it would still give only a partial idea of the whole.

The first job in making a summary is that of *selection*. Pick out the points which you think important if the summary is to be complete and correct. This cannot be done after a single reading but only after several re-readings and careful study.

The next step is to write down the main points as if they are paragraph headings for an essay and to see if they seem to be leading to a sensible report.

The third task is to write the summary, using generalization to reduce its length, that is, reducing phrases to one or two words, e.g., 'things made of iron, tin, lead, copper or brass' becomes 'metal objects' or 'a large handful of roses, carnations, stocks and snapdragons' becomes 'a bunch of flowers'.

A summary exercise is often set to test two skills in the candidate:

(a) The ability to select the most important points in a piece of writing.
(b) The ability to write good prose on a limited subject in a set number of words.

Now try the following summary

During an investigation of complaints about conditions on a housing estate, consisting of blocks of flats, a number of verbal complaints were recorded, and a questionnaire was distributed. Printed below are some of the verbal complaints, a table of answers to the questionnaire, and a list of other suggestions for improvement made by tenants. Using the material given in all three, write a report summarizing the tenants' complaints.
Your report should not exceed 170 words in length, and should consist of *two* paragraphs:
in the first, summarize complaints about the physical character and construction of the estate and the individual flats;
in the second, summarize complaints about the absence of adequate provision for the daily life of a community.

Select the materials required for each paragraph (some complaints are, of course, implied in the suggestions), and arrange them in your report clearly and coherently. Some minor complaints will have to be ignored. *Your report must be written in concise, correct English*. (Some words or expressions cannot be accurately or economically replaced, but do not copy out whole sentences or long expressions.) *State the number of words you have used*.

VERBAL COMPLAINTS
(a) 'All the blocks look alike. It's more like warehousing than rehousing.'
(b) 'It's like being in little boxes, all on top of one another.'
(c) 'We stare across the courtyard at people we don't know, and who don't know us.'
(d) 'We can't sleep for the sound of the man next door snoring.'
(e) 'The rooms are far too small – unsuitable for a family.'
(f) 'How would you like to drag a baby up six flights of stairs?'
(g) 'It takes about two hours to get enough hot water for a bath.'
(h) 'What I miss are the stalls, and a fried fish shop, and somewhere to send the children at night.'
(i) 'This place is a dump for young people. There's nowhere to go and nothing to do, so we just keep ourselves to ourselves.'

(j) 'What this place needs is a club where they have a licence to sell drink and where a man and his wife and children can all go.'

QUESTIONNAIRE

Number of answers

	Not sure	Yes	No
Is a shopping centre needed?	5	226	9
Are pram sheds needed?	23	208	9
Are bicycle sheds needed?	24	205	10
Is there enough entertainment?	30	5	205
Is a Community Centre needed?	21	216	3
Is a Church and/or Sunday-school needed?	24	212	4

OTHER SUGGESTIONS WRITTEN ON FORMS

	Number of times suggestion made
More coal bunker space	9
Drying room for washing	1
More cupboards	4
Stairs to be cleaned regularly	4
Coal to be delivered to top floors	7
A post office on the estate	26
A public house, or off-licence	47
Swimming-pool	7
Allotments	1
Children's playgrounds	12
Children's parties	2
Public transport service from the estate	11
Better footpaths	1
Health Centre and/or resident doctor	9

London GCE 'O' Level, Summer 1970

General

Draw the plan of a large bed-sitter (6 metres × 6 metres) which is to be your own for the next five years. Show the positions of the windows and the door. Then number the various items of furniture you would want in the room, such as a bed, wardrobe, desks, bookshelves, table etc. Give all these articles as a 'key' under the plan, putting only the numbers on the plan.

(a) Find out the cost of furnishing your room as shown in your plan.
(b) Find out the cost of:
   (i) carpeting the room with a good quality fitted carpet;
   (ii) with a cheap large carpet measuring 5 metres × 5 metres;
   (iii) with linoleum and two smaller 3 metres × 3 metres carpets.
(c) Your grandmother has offered to buy one luxury item for your room. What would you choose? How much would it cost?
(d) Describe the pictures or posters you could put up in your room: explain why you want them rather than other pictures and posters.
(e) Describe the colours and colour schemes for the walls, curtains, carpets and furnishings of your room.

Writing

(a) Write a newspaper advertisement for an estate of houses and flats being built in your neighbourhood, giving details of the buildings' specifications, sizes, area layout and price.
(b) Write a television commercial advertising flats being built by a company in your neighbourhood. Give details of what the viewer will see, as well as the words he will hear.

Unit 17

The Summary (2)

Now we must tackle the next steps in preparing a summary. The work already done on generalizing vocabulary goes a long way towards shortening a passage but it will not give all the reduction that is needed. More can be done by modifying and combining sentences so as to give the essential information in fewer words. Cut out unnecessary repetition, and this in itself is a great word-saver. You may find that the original material had said the same thing several times and that you need say it only once.

> This bar is reserved for members. Only members are allowed to use it. Non-members are not admitted.

In these sentences, the second and third sentences add nothing to what was said in the first.

Apart from expressing things more concisely, how much can be simply omitted from a summary? You can cut out things which are just repetitive, but you can often go further. The illustrations and examples, the figures and lists of names, can usually be generalized and not stated in full. When the full account is being written, it is very important to have definite facts and examples to back up the general assertions. The writer of the original material needs to justify his argument, while the writer of the summary needs only to state it. In this, as in everything, use the judgment of common sense. If the examples are necessary to make complete sense, keep them. Otherwise, you can reduce them to a general statement and have them in reserve to be produced if those who receive the summary demand them.

The methods used in summarizing often produce a better piece of writing than the original. Economy and precision are fundamental to good English and should be practised even in an extended treatment. Remember, however, that the improvement of style is not the main purpose of a summary. Summarizing is done to make something more quickly and easily readable. It is basically a technique for more efficient intake and not for elegance.

You can start by practising the making of a summary by reducing two or more sentences to a single sentence. Use what you have learned about generalizing, simplifying and combining. Here are some examples using single sentences which are unnecessarily long.

(a) The Company is filled with anxiety about secretaries who do their work with devotion and sincerity but are unable to express themselves clearly in writing.

i.e. The Company is worried about devoted, sincere secretaries who cannot write clearly.

(b) A notice will be placed on this notice board giving information about the place, date, time and agenda of the next meeting, before the meeting is held.

i.e. A notice on this board will give advance details of the next meeting.

When you come to summarize a longer passage or series of papers, keep in mind one very important fact: summarizing is not a mechanical reduction. If you are going to reduce 300 words to 100, this does not mean that every three words in the original will become one word in the summary, or that every three sentences will become one sentence.

This is where initial planning of the summary is necessary, so that the main ideas can be picked out and established. It will sometimes be seen that certain key sentences in the original must be retained almost as they stand. On the other hand, a paragraph which is repetitive or illustrative may be reduced to a single sentence.

Remember, too, what was said about report writing in general. It should not include anything which is not in the original and should not be so worded as to give an impression which the original does not give. Then, make a final check and compare the summary with the original. Is anything important omitted? Is anything irrelevant included?

Before going on to a fuller example of summary, here are two points which you should note and remember:

(a) The golden rule of summarizing is to try to give a fair report of the original to someone who has not seen it. Would such a person know what it was all about, without exaggeration, omission or misunderstanding? Always apply this test to your finished work.

(b) The exercises which you will be asked to do can be regarded as somewhat artificial. It is desirable to learn the basic rules for making a summary, so that they can be applied to more practical needs. Once you have mastered the technique, you can adapt it to suit your particular job or official position.

Now try the following summary exercises:

The summer of 1682, with danger to the King from Whig plots, was still a dangerous time. The London area was anything but a secure district for royal residence. A safer and pleasant place seemed to be the ancient city of Winchester. Linked to monarchy for some thousand years, it stood in a friendly countryside well dominated by royalist gentry. The heaths and glades of the New Forest were splendidly suited to the outdoor sports in which Charles II delighted. It was also conveniently close to Southampton, whence a loyal warship could easily take the King to exile.

Before the end of the year, Winchester castle was examined as a likely location. For in January of 1683 the Secretary of State sent the King's appreciation of the 'frankness' wherewith the Winchester justices (who must actually have had little choice) had shown themselves ready to part with their county's castle. The fine thirteenth-century hall of the castle was happily spared. But most of the old fortified site, along with the other ground adjacent to it, was soon available for the buildings on whose layout and design the Surveyor General must already have been at work.

By the beginning of 1683 Wren had been Surveyor General for fourteen years, and the building of royal palaces was, from the time of his visit to Paris, among his chief ambitions. But the Winchester commission was his first chance of supervising the actual erection of such a building. Predictably enough, what he proposed for the hillside above Winchester showed much French inspiration, and the palace was to be but the main element in a ceremonial layout akin to what Wren must, by 1683, have known to exist at Versailles. The exterior was to be made of red brick, with dressings of Wren's much favoured Portland stone. Behind and above the portico a flat-topped dome of the 'Mansard' type was the dominating feature. Its top would have commanded a superb view though one may doubt that warships lying over twenty miles away at Spithead would normally have been seen in the southward prospect.

As was shown in its Mansard dome, the general character of the proposed Palace was very largely French of the late seventeenth century. The feeling of pomp and splendour would have been reinforced, past a spacious forecourt, by a ceremonial avenue cutting down, through ground cleared by demolishing many houses in the city, direct to the west front of the cathedral. Somewhere in the gardens a stream let in

from the western downs would have ended in the foaming
Baroque splendour of a thirty-foot cascade.   45
 By the end of 1684 most of the outer walls had been put up
and the palace had been 'brought almost to the covering'. But,
exactly a year later, Charles was in his grave and, in the
great hall of Winchester's castle, Judge Jeffreys was at work
trying Dame Alice Lisle for her entertainment of two leading   50
followers of Monmouth in his rebellion against the new king.

B. Little *Sir Christopher Wren*

(a) In 40 words, summarize the advantages that Winchester offered as a place for King Charles to live.
(b) In 60 words, describe the main features of the palace at Winchester, if it had been built.

General

(a) Concerning the proposed palace at Winchester, what does the passage tell us about its:
   (i) siting
   (ii) layout
   (iii) materials
   (iv) style
(b) Using not more than 400 words, write a report for a guide to local housing on a building you know, pointing out:
   (i) its good features for working in;
                          in appearance;
                          in siting
   (ii) its weak features for working in;
                          in appearance;
                          in siting.
(c) Imagine that the palace of Winchester has been completed as described in the passage, and that you are guiding a group round it. Write the notes you would carry with you to help you:
   (i) to explain why the palace was built at Winchester (50 words);
   (ii) to describe the palace's external appearance (50 words).

Vocabulary

The passage contains ten words or phrases involved in building. Use a dictionary to find their meaning.

(i) ground adjacent (line 18)
  (ii) layout (line 28)
 (iii) dressings (line 30)
  (iv) Portland stone (line 31)
   (v) portico (line 31)
  (vi) 'Mansard' (line 32)
 (vii) dominating feature (line 32–3)
(viii) forecourt (line 40)
  (ix) ceremonial avenue (line 41)
   (x) Baroque splendour (line 45)

Unit 18

Summary

In Southwark, Laing has been beset by many unforeseen problems and snags during a £1.3 million housing rehabilitation programme for the borough council. 'The unknowns and extras crop up so regularly on this job that the quantity surveyor visits the site two or three times a week, whereas on new buildings he would come around about once a month,' declared the project manager for the scheme. 'Who knows what we will find when the architraves are removed or ceilings stripped? What was thought to be solid walls could be revealed to be a rotten crumbling mass that needs to be demolished and rebuilt.'

About three years ago, when Southwark first decided on rehabilitation instead of demolition, the specification called for full modernisation, including complete rewiring with new conduits chased into the walls, new soil and vent pipes and rainwater goods. Later the Council was told by the Department of the Environment to cut back as far as possible. As a result, it is replacing only essential items and re-using as much of the original material as is practicable. This has resulted in a piecemeal job with rotten wooden windows being replaced by metal, sections of guttering being inserted between existing lengths, part re-tiling of the roofs, and the strengthening of old railings. This D.o.E policy of part-replacement has produced many headaches for the builder. One was to find ways of jointing new metric-sized sewage and rainwater pipes to the existing imperial. The contractor experienced another severe setback. The long spell of continuous hot weather had turned the building into a 'tinderbox'; when a plumber went into the roof-space to cut out some pipes with an oxy-acetylene torch a spark caught the sarking and within half-an-hour the entire roof structure covering four flats was destroyed. As on the other site, the unexpected turned up frequently on the internal work. But, worst still, as soon as work commenced on the excavation of the trenches for new underground services, forgotten air raid shelters were unearthed and had to be removed. Also, in one section, the complete ground floor slab of an old factory, complete with machine bases, was discovered.

from *The Building Trades Journal*

(a) Using about 90 words, summarize the 'unforeseen problems' (lines 1–2) met with by Laing during the Southwark Borough Council 'housing rehabilitation programme' (lines 2–3).
(b) Using about 50 words, summarize the results of the Department of the Environment's order to 'cut back as far as possible' (line 17) on the housing rehabilitation programme.
(c) Imagine that you are Laing's quantity surveyor and write reports on the following incidents recorded in the passage:
    (i) finding that what appeared to be solid walls were a rotten crumbling mass needing to be demolished and rebuilt (lines 9–11).
    (ii) the destruction of the entire roof structure covering four flats by fire caused by a plumber's oxy-acetylene torch (lines 29–32).
    (iii) discovering vast concrete slabs in the ground (line 37).

Writing

(a) Write a short account for your employer on each of the following:
    (i) an unforeseen problem at your place of work.
    (ii) an emergency (such as a fire) at your place of work.
    (iii) some dangers to employees at your place of work.
(b) Write a paragraph on the advantages and disadvantages of the following for young workers on sites:
    (i) foundation digging   (v) steel erecting
    (ii) general excavating   (vii) scaffold erecting
    (iii) bulldozer driving   (viii) tile laying
    (iv) concrete pouring   (ix) plastering
    (v) bricklaying   (x) carpentering
                                (xi) outdoor painting.
(c) Write a paragraph saying why you prefer or dislike each of the following ways of working:
    (i) with people/alone;
    (ii) indoors/outdoors;
    (iii) with your mind/physical work;
    (iv) skilled/semi-skilled/unskilled;
    (v) daywork/nightwork;
    (vi) with a set wage/on piecework.

Discussion

(a) Should old buildings be saved by rehabilitation or should new buildings be put in their place?

(b) Should Council property be built and maintained only by Council building workers?

Vocabulary

Abbreviations

(a) In line 23 of the passage D.o.E. stands for the Department of the Environment. It is an abbreviation. Find out what the following abbreviations stand for:

AGM	JP	sae
CF	km	TGW
cm	Ltd	TUC
deg.	mm	vhf
e.g.	mpg	VIP
gm	mph	viz
GMT	nb	wef
GMW	OHMS	Hon. Sec.
i.e.	PAYE	inst.
pp	IOU	RIP
IQ	RSVP.	

(b) 'To cut back', on line 17 of the passage, is an expression taken from sawing and then applied to other areas of life. Explain what each of the following expressions, taken from building and applied to other areas of life, means:

    To be on the tiles
    To have a slate loose
    To raise the roof
    To go through the roof
    To cement a friendship
    To drop a brick
    To make bricks without straw
    To come down like a ton of bricks
    To get on like a house on fire
    To keep open house
    To give it house-room
    To put his house in order
    To lay it on with a trowel
    To hit the nail on the head
    To have no foundation
    To drain of energy
    To build on sand
    To be a brick.

Punctuation

The Comma

The comma (,) is used to show a small division between different parts of a sentence or to show a slight break in its construction. It indicates a less marked break than that shown by a full stop. The comma is used:
  (i) to separate items in a list, e.g. He used a hammer, nails, pliers and an axe. (No comma occurs before the final 'and' in a list.)
  (ii) to mark off exclamations, e.g. Oh, I've dropped my trowel.
  (iii) to mark off two different subjects within the same sentence, e.g. Tom bought a saw, and Jim bought a chisel.
  (iv) to mark off words which repeat, in another form, the original subject, e.g. Bill, our foreman, never uses bad language.

The serious misuse of the comma is putting it where the stronger pause of the full stop is needed, e.g. 'He went into the building, it was almost finished' is wrong.

'He went into the building. It was almost finished' is correct.

Here is an exercise to test your understanding of the comma. Correct the sentences where you consider necessary.
(a) I reached for the tea milk sugar and hot water.
(b) The house was old and decrepit, it had been empty for years.
(c) John was pleased with his rise but Jim was less happy.
(d) The growing problem of overtime, must be settled soon.
(e) The materials were poor, and were difficult to use.
(f) Oh. It has started to rain.
(g) He owns his own building firm J. Smith and Son.
(h) The solution was obvious, knock it all down.

Unit 19

Comprehension

Read the passage carefully, and then answer the questions following it.

As modern architects tell the story, the flat roof was thrust upon them by a change in technology: the development at the turn of the century of reinforced concrete. The conventional, tent-like, pitched roof had had its day but that day was gone – and good riddance. For with the pitched roof the builder was 5
stuck with a house width of about 30 ft. – the sum of two standard 20 ft. beams leaned together – and a simple rectangular or 'L' shape. By exploiting the new technology, architects could now keep pace with new uses of space and changed life-styles such as a growing desire for open-plan 10
living. The flat roof was also a first step towards turning the whole of housing design into simple geometrical shapes – and what shapes could be more suitable for mass production?

The technological argument for flat roofs was nonsense from the start. A flat roof is expensive and impractical, as it 15
entails special insulation and weather-proofing and endless difficulties in drainage. Interestingly, that other trade-mark of modernity, the flat and flush ribbon window, suffers similar headaches as it is difficult to set and to seal – which explains why it so often shows damp stains underneath. 20
Asked why his houses are so characterless, the modern architect's favourite reply is that he lacked the money for frills. How odd. In regarding an eave or a window sill as a frill, he is throwing money away.

As for the mass-production argument, this turned out to be 25
a red herring – and a dangerous one. The success of prefabrication doesn't depend on simplified geometrical sections (one of the early successes, Hobart House, was neo-Georgian), but on the degree of standardisation. Alas, whatever could be gained by pre-fab was lost dozens of times over 30
in teething pains and delay. Costs got steadily worse. The supply of men and materials was thrown out of kilter – and with devastating effect: losing a generation of bricklayers, for example, when the fashion changed to poured concrete. Even more belatedly the architects rediscovered an old truth: 35
that vernacular housing has *always* had standardised parts

and, what is more, a built-in system for innovation that works by giving the proven the benefit of the doubt. But here there is another puzzle: if the case for pre-fab was failing so miserably, why were architects so determined to support it 40 long after its cause had been lost? It provides them with work. As long as housing stays conventional, then the architect is out in the cold: housebuilding goes on as it has gone on for centuries with little or no professional help. But let the design radically change – or 45 better still let radical change in design be joined to radical change in technology – and the architect comes into his own.

Conrad Jameson *The Sunday Times Magazine*

According to the passage, what are:
(a) the limitations placed on houses by a pitched roof (line 4),
(b) the advantages claimed by architects for the flat roof (line 11),
(c) the disadvantages of the flat roof,
(d) the faults and bad effects of pre-fabricated building (lines 26–7)?

Summary

Summarize the following passage about automation and its effects in industry generally, using not more than 140 words.

It is widely recognised that we must automate our industry or else we shall find ourselves unable to compete. But the technical changes in the field of automation are so rapid that it is difficult for anyone not directly involved to understand them and what they imply. One cannot reasonably expect the average Member of Parliament, mainly concerned as he is bound to be with the many day-to-day problems of his constituency, to go much more deeply into the subject than to examine the likely effect of automation upon employment and therefore on voting, in his area. Yet, fortunately, politics are not only the concern of politicians but necessarily involve the general mass of citizens. It is an urgent political task to educate the people as a whole so as to make them aware of the broad problems and the opportunities of automation.

With the support of public opinion we must strive for a national policy on this issue. One of the bases on which such a policy ought to rest is an organization, perhaps set up jointly by government, industry and trade unions, which would unite sociologists, engineers, economists, experts on labour relations and psychologists, and would engage in a vigorous drive to make people understand the full implications of automation. It should aim at presenting a fair picture, so that the whole problem could be viewed in perspective, from the point of view of the individual, the community and the nation. The man in the street must be given the opportunity to know what is happening, and why, and what part he should play in it.

This type of organization would remind industrial workers, for instance, that the mechanical handling of materials has greatly reduced accidents and that ill-health can arise from contact with toxic substances; in other words, that there are many processes more safely done by machines. But it would show that it was well aware of the human problems involved in replacing physical effort by increased responsibility. The fact that not all workers can accept the kind of responsibility which automation would place upon them should not be passed over. The organization would urge the necessity of careful selection of workers, in order to prevent nervous fatigue and possible breakdown. It would provide objective and well-informed long-term forecasts of the types of skill which were likely to be in increasing demand and those which were likely to wither away.

(a) All the following technical terms occur in the opening passage. Explain what each one is.

(i) architects (line 1)
(ii) reinforced concrete (line 3)
(iii) pitched roof (line 4)
(iv) standard beams (line 7)
(v) open-plan living (line 10)
(vi) mass production (line 13)
(vii) insulation (line 16)
(viii) weather-proofing (line 16)
(ix) drainage (line 17)
(x) ribbon window (line 18)
(xi) eave (line 23)
(xii) pre-fabrication (line 26)
(xiii) neo-Georgian (line 28)
(xiv) poured concrete (line 34)
(xv) vernacular housing (line 36)

(b) Here are other technical terms associated with the building industry. Explain what each one is.

(i) architrave
(ii) corbel
(iii) interstice
(iv) jamb
(v) load-bearing
(vi) joist
(vii) sofit
(viii) ties
(ix) estate agent
(x) estimator
(xi) planner
(xii) sub-contracter
(xiii) surveyor
(xiv) valuer

(c) Certain phrases are used in the opening passage, not with their actual meaning ('literal') but with a special use ('figurative'). Explain what these phrases mean, as they are used in the passage.

   (i) trade-mark (line 17)
   (ii) red herring (line 26)
   (iii) teething pains (line 31)
   (iv) out of kilter (line 32)
   (v) out in the cold (line 43)

Here are other figurative expressions taken from the building industry. Explain what each one means:

   (i) to drop a brick
   (ii) to leave no stone unturned
   (iii) to get blood out of a stone
   (iv) to get to the top of the ladder
   (v) to wind up an affair
   (vi) to have an axe to grind
   (vii) to call a spade a spade
   (viii) to throw a spanner in the works
   (ix) to slip through your fingers
   (x) to pull your weight
   (xi) to wash your hands of
   (xii) to pump for information
   (xiii) a dead-end
   (xiv) too big for his boots
   (xv) as broad as it is long
   (xvi) a chip off the old block
   (xvii) the thin end of the wedge
   (xviii) rule of thumb.

(d) Some proverbs (sayings that contain general, useful experience) are taken from the building industry. Explain what each of the following proverbs means:
   (i) Rome was not built in a day.
   (ii) You can't make bricks without straw.
   (iii) People who live in glass houses should not throw stones.

Unit 20

Comprehension

Read the following, and then attempt the questions arising from it.

No building type today fulfils the same functions as a castle, and thus no building has the same complex design criteria. The castle, unknown before the Norman Conquest, was essentially architectural propaganda. It was built to dominate the people of a district. All facets of life, religious, civil, military, educational and political, were conducted literally in its shadow. 5

The accommodation which a castle had to provide included a Royal residence, administration offices, courts, military barracks, and stores for arms, food and livestock, etc. It is likely that the majority of this accommodation, unless the castle was under siege, was provided by buildings within the courtyard of the castle. 10

Perhaps the most important design requirement of the castle, and the one which marks it out from the majority of other buildings which survive from this period, is the speed required of construction. Whilst the building of a cathedral might well take the work of a generation or more, if a castle was to fulfil its military function it was needed quickly. This factor as much as any other probably determined the design of Rhuddlan Castle. Rhuddlan was substantially completed in less than three years and even a short walk around the considerable ruins reveals this to be a remarkable achievement even by today's standards. Though the 13th century building industry was not hampered by the current machinery of legislation and the division between design and construction, the completion of a first-order castle in such a short time stretches the imagination. 15 20 25

Even at Rhuddlan, the castle did not comprise the entire project. Plans were being made to enclose the adjacent town by a town wall and, perhaps more significantly, before building of the castle could properly begin, a channel three miles long had to be cut to divert and deepen the River Clywd and render it navigable both for seaborne forces and the transport of materials to support the building programme. Yet despite this, and despite the considerable problems of communi- 30 35 cation which must have arisen because of language differences and the doubtless constant guerilla activity, the work upon the castle, which began in spring of 1278, was completed, apart from some final finishes, by autumn 1280. By November of 1280 the building team had moved on to the next project!

Dr. A. J. Wilson *Building Technology and Management*

(a) Why does no building type today fulfil 'the same functions as a castle' (line 1)?
(b) What is meant by 'architectural propaganda' (line 4)?
(c) What was 'the most important design requirement of the castle' (line 14)?
(d) What is meant by 'substantially completed' (line 21)?
(e) Why was Rhuddlan castle 'a remarkable achievement even by today's standards' (lines 23–4)?
(f) What was the first work done at the Rhuddlan site?

Summary

(a) Why was it possible to build Rhuddlan in three years? (Use 50 words.)
(b) What problems were met during the building of Rhuddlan castle? (Use 50 words.)
(c) What were the uses of castles such as Rhuddlan in the Middle Ages? (Use 50 words.)

Discussion

(a) Should old buildings be preserved?
(b) What are the best ways of saving old buildings?
(c) Which modern buildings have been built as 'architectural propaganda'?
(d) What kinds of laws should govern building projects?
(e) Which materials are (i) the most interesting, (ii) the most dangerous to work with today?
(f) How can lasting workmanship be ensured today?
(g) When is guerilla warfare justified?
(h) Is society still basically the same as in the Middle Ages?

Writing

(a) Describe three buildings you have seen which have 'stretched your imagination'. Describe how you would fortify some building you know to withstand armed attack.
(b) How would you organize the building of a small brick garden shed?

Essay writing

You will have to show yourself able to do two types of writing: the imaginative and the practical. The first requires you to invent a story or description. The second requires you to present facts or discussion in a clear and readable way.

For both types of writing you should remember the following:
(a) Where there is a choice of topics, choose your subject carefully. Select the one you know most about, so that you can develop it in an interesting way.
(b) Study the chosen title carefully to determine whether it would make a better story, description or discussion.
(c) Assemble as many ideas about your chosen topic as you can and organize these into a plan which will give an overall shape to your writing. Shape out your essay into paragraphs leading from the beginning to an end.
(d) Work out a good opening and ending. Consider a number of alternative openings which would encourage a reader to go on and endings which would leave a reader satisfied.
(e) Keep looking at your title to make sure that what you are writing is relevant to it and that you are keeping to the point.
(f) Watch the quality of your writing and ask yourself if your sentences are varied and correct; the words lively and interesting, or, at least, not old hackneyed phrases; your examples and comparisons fitting.
(g) Watch the accuracy of your writing and ask yourself if your spelling is accurate, your punctuation correct, your sentences truly constructed and your paraphrasing sound, so that each one is self-contained and leads to the next.

When you do all these things you should be almost certain of producing worthwhile essays. Here are more titles inspired by this unit's passage. Write an essay on one of the following:
(a) The ruin.
(b) The haunted castle.

(c) The siege.
(d) 'Castles in the air'.
(e) On being 'King of the castle'.
(f) Imagine that you have bought a small castle and its grounds. Describe how you would adapt it to become either:
   (i) a stately home; or
   (ii) a safari park.
(g) The dungeon.
(h) Is the 'Englishman's home his castle' today?

Letter writing

You have been asked by your local Conservation Society to inspect your local castle to see what repairs are necessary, and at what expense, as they have been offered it free by its present owner. The Conservation Society are interested in developing the castle and its grounds as a tourist attraction or some kind of museum or pleasure grounds. Write letters, as follows:
(a) to your local Mayor trying to enlist interest and help;
(b) to a local builder asking about costs and the availability of various materials you will need;
(c) to a friend explaining what you are doing and what you hope to do.

Unit 21

Comprehension

Read the following passage; then answer the questions below.

In the past, site huts were built of wood, corrugated iron and even canvas stretched on a rigid frame. Sanitary arrangements were primitive, and facilities for washing down or food preparation were unheard of.

The trend today is towards a generation of purpose-built units fulfilling any required function, which can be installed on site with the minimum of fuss. They may be bought or hired depending on individual circumstances, and offer a great many advantages over the traditional wooden hutting.

Unlike conventional hutting, purpose-built mobile site accommodation is delivered pre-erected, thus cutting out the need to use expensive site labour. Modern units are fully finished with good insulation, and can be easily moved once on site.

Shelter has been a basic requirement since man first found the weather to be an alien force. If the building industry is to prosper by recruiting good quality staff, then good shelter remains a basic site requirement. Men must be able to dress, eat and rest in dry, warm conditions. Modern site accommodation manufacturers make this possible through a wide variety of chassis, jack and skid-mounted units, some of them tailored to specific site requirements, others drawn from comprehensive stocks.

Proper sanitary arrangements are now mandatory on building sites – gone are the bad old days when a screen trench would suffice. Site toilets – whether they rely on chemical waste disposal or are connected to the main sewers – must be adequate in relation to the number of men employed and should offer privacy and washing facilities. Depending on the size of site, toilets can now be supplied individually or in multiple blocks. Most are now supplied with low-level suites, individual wash-hand basins, and come completely wired for connection to site electricity supply or generator.

All sites are different and some call for specialised accommodation. Where there is existing craning, skid or jack-mounted units can be easily positioned. Occasionally, how-

ever, it may be more convenient to use chassis-mounted
accommodation which may be towed into position. There is
also sometimes a need to move accommodation units from   40
site to site, and here truly mobile units have the advantage.

from *Building Technology and Management*

(a) What does the author mean by the following words: 'traditional' (line 9); 'conventional' (line 10); 'insulation' (line 13); 'mandatory' (line 24); 'mobile' (line 41)?
(b) What do you understand by 'purpose-built units' (line 5)?
(c) When the author says (line 8) that the units may be bought or hired depending on 'individual circumstances', what sort of individual circumstances do you think he has in mind?
(d) What do you understand by 'expensive site labour' (line 12)? Why should it be expensive?
(e) What does the author mean by speaking of the weather as an 'alien force' (line 16)? What is meant when we say that a person is an alien? What do the two uses of the word have in common?
(f) Some of the units, we are told (line 22) are 'tailored to specific site requirements'; in your own words, explain how others are supplied.
(g) Rewrite more simply 'must be adequate in relation to the number of men employed' (line 28).
(h) Explain 'specialized (site) accommodation' (line 35).
(i) In the first paragraph, the author says that in the past, sanitary arrangements were primitive; where, later, does he give an example of this? Why is the example 'primitive' (line 3)?
(j) In 2–3 sentences for each, explain the advantages to (i) management and (ii) the employees, of the units the author describes.
(k) Explain clearly the difference between chassis, jack and skid-mounted units. If you do not understand the terms, try to find out from another source.
(l) Why can skid and jack-mounted units only be erected where there is existing craning?
(m) According to the passage, what is needed in a good site hut? How does a modern unit supply these needs?
(n) If you have worked on a building site, describe the sort of facilities that were provided; say whether you think they were adequate or not, and why.

Writing

(a) Describe a wet day on a building site: pay attention to its appearance and how the rain affects the workmen.

(b) Describe the appearance and facilities of a good site accommodation unit that you have seen or heard about.

(c) Write a radio or television sketch set in a building site hut entitled:
- (i) a personal argument;
- (ii) a political argument;
- (iii) monday morning, first thing;
- (iv) friday evening, last thing.

Do not forget to put in directions for what the viewer sees, or sound effects for the listener.

Describe how to:
- (i) erect a small wooden shed;
- (ii) erect a wooden fence;
- (iii) lay down (crazy) paving;
- (iv) repoint a house's walls;
- (v) make concrete;
- (vi) make mortar.

(e) All the following terms may be heard at a meeting in a site hut. Explain what each of them means:
- (i) an agenda;
- (ii) a quorum;
- (iii) a point of order;
- (iv) standing orders;
- (v) a card-vote;
- (vi) a show of hands;
- (vii) a casting vote.

(f) Write out messages, to be given over the phone by some person other than yourself, for each of the following situations. Remember that your message should be as short as possible yet include all the essential information:
- (i) to your employer explaining why you will not be at work that morning;
- (ii) to your family explaining why you will be late home that evening;
- (iii) to the police telling of an emergency on the site;
- (iv) to your union's local office explaining a dispute at work.

(g) Write out messages to be taken by hand:
- (i) to the stores asking for extra building material and explaining why it is needed;
- (ii) to your foreman explaining why you have had to leave the site;

(iii) to your employer explaining a grievance on behalf of all your workmates.
(h) Write out the notes you would need to refer to in order to give the following short talks. Remember that notes should be written large enough to be read at a distance and not so fully that they become a 'read' speech.
  (i) To senior pupils at your old school, describing your first year of work and/or of Further Education.
  (ii) To your workmates, urging them to strike, or not to strike, over rates of pay.
  (iii) To your employer, when you lead a deputation of your workmates to ask for better site accommodation.
  (iv) At a union meeting, making the case that hard manual jobs deserve the same rewards as managerial and professional ones.

Vocabulary

(a) Sometimes there are two or more meanings for a word spelled and spoken in the same way. All the following occur in the passage and you are asked to write down two or more of each of their meanings.

iron (line 1)	rest (line 19)
even (line 2)	jack (line 21)
frame (line 2)	drawn (line 22)
down (line 3)	stocks (line 23)
can (line 6)	screen (line 25)
may (line 7)	main (line 27)
over (line 9)	relation (line 28)
force (line 16)	size (line 30)
staff (line 17)	craning (line 36)

(b) All the following words of the same type occur in the building industry. What are the two meanings of each?

bay	joint
bit	mortar
board	nail
brace	pen
chisel	pick
clippers	plane
drill	point
fall	rail
file	ruler
foot	swing
grain	vice

(c) Some words are spelled differently but are said the same. Each of the following occurs in the passage and you are asked to give its alternative spelling and meaning:

canvas (line 2)   waste (line 27)
hired (line 8)   main (line 27)
great (line 9)   more (line 38)
weather (line 16)   sometimes (line 40)
some (line 21)   need (line 40)

(d) Each of the following words of the same type occurs in the building industry. Find their alternative spelling and meaning:

board   ceiling
draught   gauge
jamb   key
plain   stair

(e) Some words are spelled alike but said differently, so that the spelling can have two meanings, depending on pronunciation. Find the two pronunciations and meanings of the following:

content   minute
convict   object
desert   polish
invalid   refuse

Unit 22

Comprehension

Read the following passage, and then answer the questions following it.

Architectural tradition is based upon the wall accepted as the main support of the building structure. The walls of the past, being structural, were designed to express massiveness, and the solidity was accentuated by infrequent piercing and deep reveals. The expression of the wall as a thin sheathing, of no more structural importance than the window, is a result of modern constructional methods. The function of the wall has changed; it is a thin skin, hung on a framework instead of standing on a foundation. 'It represents a change in architectural method more profound than any previous structural invention', and we see that where the modern purpose of the wall is understood there is a revolution in the design of the facade. The wall surface is regarded, aesthetically, as a continuous plane; as a skin enveloping and expressing the surface of a volume.

The placing and size of windows are no longer governed by the requirements of symmetry; the glass becomes part of the continuous enveloping membrane, flush with the outer face, and the contrast between window and wall surface, which tends to emphasise the massiveness of the wall, is much reduced by this arrangement. The character is expressed rather by the material and the disposition of the parts of the surface than by scale and proportion in the accepted traditional sense.

Smooth stucco has desirable aesthetic qualities as a surfacing material, but it is subject to crazing and discolouration, and, though much experimental work has been done in an attempt to produce a non-crazing rendering, the perfect cement surface has yet to be found.

Where expense does not prohibit the use of stone and marbles, these natural materials may be employed, purely as facings, applied not in imitation of masonry construction but in thin slabs with fine unbroken joints, that do not produce the illusion of bonding, but emphasise the continuity of the surface in sizes that keep the scale of the plate glass of the windows, and finished to a similar smooth glass texture.

Brick is not, aesthetically, the best material for the filling wall; laid conventionally it suggests mass, but economically it remains the most satisfactory proven surfacing material in general use. Attempts have been made to emphasise con- *40* tinuity of surface by suppressing as much as possible the bonding pattern, and by the use of mortar coloured to match the surface of the brick.

F. R. S. Yorke *The Modern House*

(a) What kinds of reader could this article be written for?
(b) According to the article, how has the 'function of the wall' changed (line 7)?
(c) According to the passage, how is the 'character' of the wall expressed (line 21)?
(d) What examples does the author offer of the different 'expressions' of walls?
(e) What are the advantages and limitations of the different wall 'expressions'?
(f) Is the writer more concerned with the technical problems of building houses or is he more concerned with the discussing of a building's attraction of appearance? Or is he concerned with both equally? Give evidence to support your answers.

Vocabulary

(a) The passage is full of technical words. Explain what is meant by each of the following:

   (i) piercing (line 4)   (xii) stucco (line 25)
  (ii) reveals (line 5)   (xiii) aesthetic (line 25)
 (iii) sheathing (line 5)   (xiv) surfacing material (lines 25–6)
 (iv) skin (line 8)   (xv) crazing (line 26)
  (v) framework (line 8)   (xvi) facings (line 32)
 (vi) facade (line 13)   (xvii) masonry construction (line 32)
 (vii) symmetry (line 17) (xviii) slabs (line 33)
(viii) membrane (line 18) (xix) bonding (line 34)
 (ix) flush (line 18)   (xx) texture (line 36)
  (x) scale (line 23)   (xxi) filling wall (lines 37–8)
 (xi) proportion (line 23)

(b) 'Proven' (line 39) is a word of American use that has come into English in place place of 'proved'. American terms are coming into English all the time, e.g. OK, guy, groovy. What are the English words for the following American terms?

   (i) bill   (iv) cookie   (vii) fall
  (ii) candy   (v) crackers (viii) fawcett
 (iii) checkers (vi) dumb   (ix) freshman

(x) gas	(xv) mad	(xx) sidewalk
(xi) grip	(xvi) pants	(xxi) sneakers
(xii) hog	(xvii) pavements	(xxii) steer
(xiii) hood	(xviii) porch	(xxiii) stenographer
(xiv) lumber	(xix) raise	(xxiv) vest

(c) Try out the following word-games in the group or on the site:
 (i) See how many words you can make using only the letters of 'Constantinople'.
 (ii) Head-to-tail, in which each word begins with the last letter of the word before it, e.g. George – Edward – Duncan.
 In three minutes see how many words in this chain you can make from words relating to the following: construction work, football teams, pop stars.
 (iii) Word squares, in which four four-letter words are arranged in the form of a square. The square must read the same from left to right and from top to bottom, e.g.
 KING
 IDOL
 NORA
 GLAD
 (iv) Anagrams, in which a word is formed by re-ordering all the letters in it into another word, e.g. 'slate' becomes 'tales'. Write anagrams for:
 inch, least, among, elbow, thorn, hire, bores, nails, feels.

Punctuation

Full Stops
There are three kinds of 'full stop' used to mark the end of a sentence. These are the full stop (.), the exclamation mark (!) and the question mark (?). All three indicate the end of a complete statement and the first word following them always has a capital letter, e.g. Watch out! My hammer has fallen.

A *full stop* is used to show the end of a complete statement, which may be any number of words, e.g. Phone this number. Ask for the shop steward. Go.

An *exclamation mark* is used to show that words, phrases or sentences are said in a tone of marked surprise, delight or anger, e.g. Ouch! What a way to lay bricks!

A *question mark* is used to show that the final rising tone of questioning is present in the words written, e.g. What? Where is the foreman at the moment?

Points to note
Far too often writing is spoiled by commas being used where full stops should go.
 The following is wrong: The boss is coming, you had better go.
 The following is correct: The boss is coming. You had better go.
 Far too often writing is spoiled by necessary full stops being left out.
 The following is wrong: There was a meeting at the site when I got there no one was about for several minutes I waited to see if people would turn up.
 The following is correct: There was a meeting at the site. When I got there no one was about. For several minutes I waited to see if people would turn up.

Use plenty of full stops, even after a few words.

Punctuate the following, using full stops, exclamation marks or question marks, to give a different reading to each sentence:
(a) Don't forget the windows look out over there.
(b) He fell from the roof through a trap door he smashed.
(c) Place it in the concrete paint when it is dry.
(d) What do you think I'm giving money away.
(e) How cautiously the Red Indians greet one another.
(f) They cancelled the order for the gates we had finished at last.
(g) This concrete will never set rock hard until you succeed.
(h) We all missed him with a stone we each contributed to his memory.

Unit 23

Technical diagrams

Under Article 3 of the Town and Country Planning General Development Order 1973, enlargements, alterations, and improvements to a private dwelling house may be carried out without express planning permission from the Local Planning Authority provided they meet certain conditions.

SIZE: A proposal must not enlarge the overall size of the house by more than 50 cubic metres although in the case of a larger house it is possible to extend the dwelling by up to 1/10 of the original, up to a maximum of 115 cubic metres.
In calculating the cubic content, measurements should be taken externally. In deciding whether a particular proposal is 'permitted development', previous extensions, including garages, must be taken into account unless they were built as part of the original house or were added before July 1948.

POSITION: Any addition or extension, including a garage, must not project beyond the forward-most part of any wall of the house which faces onto a highway.

HEIGHT: The height of any addition or extension must not extend above the highest part of the roof of the original dwelling house.

(a) The following diagrams show proposed extensions to existing property (shaded areas represent proposed extensions or extensions added after July 1948).

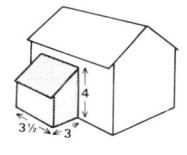

Fig. 1 Rear extension under 50 cubic metres with no previous extensions, so planning permission is not required (unless there is a road at the back of the house).

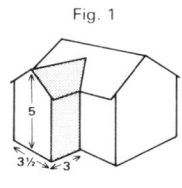

Fig. 2

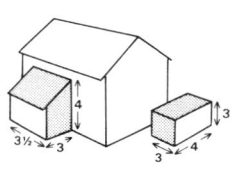

Fig. 3

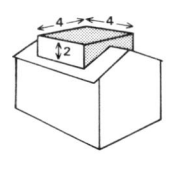

Fig. 4

Indicate briefly, following the model for Fig. 1, why planning permission is or is not required before building the proposed extension. In cases where there is some unknown factor which may influence the situation, indicate this in brackets, as in the example given. All measurements shown are in metres.

(b) The following are four further descriptions by the author of the above material of examples of proposed extensions to private dwelling houses which do, or do not, require planning permission. Draw a simple sketch, such as that which appears in question (a) to illustrate each description.

   (i) Dormer extension under 50 cubic metres and does not increase the height of the roof, so provided that no other extensions have been carried out, planning permission is not required.

  (ii) Extension at the side of the house which, although under 50 cubic metres, projects in front of the forwardmost part of the wall which faces a highway, so planning permission is required.

 (iii) Extension at the side of a corner house. Under 50 cubic metres and does not project in front of the house, *but* because it projects in front of a wall which faces a highway (in this case, a side wall) planning permission is required.

 (iv) Extension at the side of a corner house enlarging existing garage which was built as a later addition to the original house. Some of the existing and proposed extensions exceed 50 cubic metres so planning permission is required.

K. R. Fines for Brighton Planning Department,
Extending Your Home

Punctuation (revision)

The following extract comes from the same booklet as the previous material in this unit. Punctuation is omitted, but oblique strokes show where it should be inserted. Copy out the passage, inserting in pencil the punctuation you think is appropriate (only full stops and commas are required, although in at least one instance a semi-colon could be used).

Generally/ semi-detached houses are built as matching

pairs/ using the same detailing and materials and it is important to make sure that a new extension does not disturb the symmetrical design of the houses/ with a two-storey extension at the side of the house/ the appearance may often be improved by incorporating a pitched or hipped roof/ this also helps to integrate the new with the existing work/ where an extension is to be built on the side of the house/ it should normally be set back from the front wall of the existing building/ the correct distance will depend on the characteristics of the particular house/ it could be as much as one metre or as little as 10 centimetres depending on the particular circumstances/ setting the new part back slightly helps to overcome the unsightly 'matching-in' of the brickwork into the existing walls/ it also creates an interesting contrast by means of shadows cast by the original building/

When you have written out the passage, read it aloud to a friend, or into a recorder (as you did in the Punctuation exercise in Unit 7), and try to determine whether your punctuation is correct according to whether your voice rises or falls. Having listened carefully, amend the punctuation you have already inserted if you think it necessary, and complete it in ink. You may find it easier to work in pairs, trying to ensure that your final versions agree.

Letter writing and form filling

Suppose that you are thinking of building an extension to the house in which you are at present living. Before starting work on it you would need to fill in Planning Application and Building Regulation forms.

(a) Write to your local Planning Department asking for a supply of these forms. Explain that you need them for an exercise on a TEC Construction course.
(b) Fill in each of the forms correctly.
(c) Draw up rough plans, bearing in mind the conditions and advice given in the extracts above, and work out whether you would need planning permission.
(d) Draft the letter you would send to the Planning Department to accompany the forms and plans. Either explain that you think the extensions will not need planning permission and indicate why, but ask them to confirm this; or refer to the fact that planning permission will be required, but explain clearly why you think it should be given.

Unit 24

Comprehension

Read the following passage; and then answer the questions following it.

He went back into the cathedral, and stood in the south transept, for already there was less dust in the air, and what there was, hung diminishing. The delvers no longer worked with cloth over their mouths, nor was there a pillar of dust over them. Only their heads and the upthrown shovels were 5
visible. When the shovels fell, they did not ring on rubble but cut with a soft scrape and chunk; and a hodman was carrying away a hodful of dark earth. But it was not the hodman or the delvers who interested him, for Roger Mason stood on the farther side of the pit, looking down, and his eyes were star- 10
ing.

Jocelin stood on the lip of the pit and spoke to the master builder.

'Well, Roger? Are you satisfied?'

The master builder neither answered him nor looked at 15
him. He spoke down the pit.

'Use the prod,' he said, 'and dig. Anything?'

'Nothing, master. Come-hup!'

A man's head appeared and his two hands. He held the iron rod in both of them, one thumb marking a distance, the other 20
on the shining point. The master builder inspected the rod slowly from one thumb to the other. He looked through Jocelin, shaped his lips to whistle but made no sound.

Jocelin said, 'A miracle. You've seen the foundations; or rather, the lack of them.' 25

There was contempt and amusement in the master builder's laugh.

'The foundations are there. They are just enough for a building of this weight. Look, you can see what they did. Follow the side of the pit down. Rubble down to there, and 30
then something more; then nothing but mud. They made a raft of brushwood and piled the filling on top. And even that isn't certain. There must be gravel under here somewhere, and it must come near the surface; *must* come near the surface, or I don't know my business. Perhaps there was a bank, 35
a reef the river left. That mud down there may be no more than a pocket of dirt.'

Jocelin laughed down over his nose delightedly. His chin lifted.

'Yet your craft can find nothing certain, my son. You say 40
they built a raft. Why not believe the building floats on it? It's simpler to believe in a miracle.'

William Golding The Spire

(a) Why was there 'less dust in the air' (line 2)?
(b) What did it mean to the builders when the shovels 'did not ring on rubble' (line 6)?
(c) Why did Jocelin ask Roger, 'Are you satisfied?' (line 14)?
(d) What was Roger hoping to hear in reply to his question, 'Anything?' (line 17)?
(e) What did the iron rod with 'one thumb marking a distance' (line 20) indicate?
(f) Why did the master builder 'shape his lips to whistle' (line 23)?
(g) What is the 'miracle' (line 24)?
(h) How does the master builder explain the building's foundations?

Attempt the following exercises about new buildings today.
(a) Your Authority is at present planning to build a new school – the Osborne Willoughby High School – which will also be used as a community centre. It is being planned in two phases; plans for Phase 1 are already complete and will provide for normal requirements for school use.

Phase 2 will provide sports facilities for both school and community. The Committee set up to organize the planning of the school building is to report to the Council shortly, and you are asked to draw up a table showing the proposed accommodation of Phase 2. The Borough Architect hands you the following information and asks you to include it all in the table:

Building will be in 3 (perhaps 4) groups.

Group 1 will include first-aid facilities (3×3), and office (3×3), staff and general toilets ($2 \times 3, 6 \times 3$), entrance hall (10×3) and cleaners' store (8×3). The general toilets will have to contain vending machines.

Group 2 will have a parents' room overlooking the pool, and a quiet room and a games room, both overlooking the sports area (3×12), (6×10), (6×10). There'll be a bar area and a bar store in this Group, and also a drinking area ($4 \times 12, 6 \times 12$). The bar store and area must have access from the road, and the drinking area will overlook the pool.

Group 3 will be the Pool Hall. The pool will be 24×12 with a

6-metre surround. In addition, there will be changing rooms which will include facilities for disabled people. The changing rooms will include locker space, pre-wash facilities and toilets, all designed so that the relative amount of space alloted to male and female areas can be adjusted at any time according to the sex ratio required. Dimensions – 16 × 12.

Group 4 is still under consideration. If it is decided to include this group in the plans it will accommodate at least 3 squash courts with a total area of 200m^2. But we're hoping to make this a commercial operation, and if so we should need 6 courts and the operators would require professional rooms, clubroom, and a manager's flat at least.

The Borough Architect adds: 'When you draw up the table, will you show the area, as well as the dimensions for each space listed, and the total area for each group? Measurements are in metres, but I'd like them shown, too, in Imperial Measure – not everyone is familiar with metric systems yet. A metre is just over 39 inches, but don't try to be too accurate – we only want to give people a general idea of the size. Generally you can assume that 10 metres is 33 feet, 6 metres is 20 feet.'

(b) Assume that the Authority for which you work has recently acquired a large and attractive building, with about 300 acres of surrounding land, for use by schools and youth groups as a recreation and activity centre; you are appointed to act as the Warden's Assistant, or as his Secretary.

The Centre will accommodate a maximum of 60 students with 6 staff or group leaders in comfortable but not luxurious quarters. While it will provide teaching and indoor recreation facilities, it will operate mainly as an outdoors pursuit centre.

A leaflet is being devised to send out to all enquiries. You are asked to draft the section of the leaflet giving details of the facilities offered (both inside and outside) and the types of activities which can be followed at the centre, together with the centre's particular advantages having regard to the nature of the countryside in which it is set.

You may base your description on an area with which you are familiar but provide a fictional name for the Centre.

from *OND Public Administration English, June 1975*

Punctuation

Direct Speech

If you use speech as part of a story or description, it is important that you punctuate it correctly. The best way to learn direct speech punctuation is to keep alert when you are reading. Note how the conversation is punctuated in the passage at the opening of Unit 24.

The following points will give you the main rules for punctuating direct speech.

(a) Actual words spoken by a person in a story are enclosed by quotation marks. Quotation marks (also called inverted commas) may be single or double. It does not matter which you use, so long as you are consistent. The passage in this unit uses single quotation marks.

'Well, Roger? Are you satisfied?' are the actual words Jocelin spoke, and they are, therefore, enclosed in quotation marks.

(b) The first word spoken has a capital letter, even if it comes in the middle of a sentence, e.g. Jocelin said, 'A miracle.'

(c) When a sentence spoken by someone is broken in the middle *by a verb of saying*, the continuation of the sentence does not re-begin with a capital letter, e.g. 'Use the prod,' he said, 'and dig. Anything?'

N.B. A comma is needed before quoted words, if these begin in the middle of a sentence, as above.

(d) Punctuation marks, which show how the spoken words are said, are placed inside the quotation marks, e.g. 'Nothing, master. Come-hup!'

(e) It is usual to begin a new paragraph every time there is a new speaker. See the passage at the beginning of this unit.

(f) Quotation marks are also placed around:
  (i) quotations from books, films, etc., e.g. 'A pillar of dust' is a very vivid phrase.
  (ii) titles of books and films, e.g. 'The Spire' is about the building of a medieval cathedral spire.
  (iii) words used in a special way, e.g. 'Delver' is no longer generally used in English.

Put in quotation marks, where necessary, in the following sentences.
(a) The foreman said who's got the time sheets.
(b) You should have phoned shouted the boss if you were going to be late.

(c) Can I borrow your hammer I asked.
(d) That is disappointing he said your work is below standard.
(e) Have you seen my copy of The Spire.
(f) To be or not to be was written by Shakespeare.
(g) Watch your head he shouted.
(h) A carpenter whispered can you spare some pliers.
(i) Golding uses many old words such as hodman.
(j) Get off the site he shouted.

Unit 25

Comprehension

Read the following passage; then answer the questions following it.

In his first housing speech Bevan protested against the whole pre-war system of building; it produced 'castrated communities'. The arrangement whereby the speculative builders built for one income group and the local authorities for another was, 'a wholly evil thing from a civilized point of view, a monstrous infliction upon the essential one-ness of the community'. Local authorities had been left to provide 'twilight villages' whereas the speculative builders were responsible for 'the fretful fronts stretching along the great roads out of London', belonging to what he understood was called 'the marzipan period'. The local authorities could never do worse, and, given the chance of architectural diversification, they should do much better.

Much wider municipal ownership could offer a tentative solution to these complexities. By the same reasoning, local authorities should strive to find hospitality for all age groups on their estates. 'I hope that the old people will not be asked to live in colonies of their own – they don't want to look out of their windows on endless processions of the funerals of their friends; they also want to look at processions of perambulators.'

Many of his hopes were disappointed and for an obvious reason: the interests of speed often conflicted with those of wise siting, and in those years speed was bound to win the day. Yet within the ambit where Bevan's writ ran, he applied his principle in practice: he insisted on good standards, particularly when it came from those who would faint from claustrophobia in 900 square feet. And, to anticipate the story, nothing made him sadder than when his successor as Housing Minister, Hugh Dalton, surrendered to the clamour.

One of the oddities of Britain's post-war housing history is that the best houses were built in the first five years when the stringency was greatest, and that only after this most testing period was the great post-war opportunity lost to forbid the re-growth of giant working-class ghettoes. Fortunately, standards have not been universally depressed to the level encouraged by the Ministry in London after 1951, but, for that, the credit is due to local authorities who acquired better habits in those first ambitious years.

Michael Foot *Aneurin Bevan*, Volume 2

(a) According to the passage, what was the 'pre-war system of building' (line 2) to which Bevan objected?
(b) What did Bevan mean by the 'one-ness of the community' (line 6–7)?
(c) Why did Bevan want 'much wider municipal ownership' (line 14)?
(d) According to the passage, why were many of Bevan's hopes 'disappointed' (line 22)?
(e) What examples of Bevan's 'good standards' (line 26) are given in the passage?
(f) According to the passage, what faults developed in council housing after Bevan ceased to be the Housing Minister?
(g) (i) Who is the present Minister responsible for housing in this country?
    (ii) Who is the Chairman of your local council Housing Committee? Who are the members of the committee?
    (iii) What is your local council's policy about council housing now, and in the future?
    (iv) How does one set about obtaining a council flat or house? What rules of age and residence apply?
    (v) How does one set about buying one's own flat or house? What rules of age and income apply?
    (vi) What are: a conservation area; a scheduled building; a development zone?

Punctuation

The Apostrophe

In the passage in Unit 25, the apostrophe occurs in both its uses:
(a) to denote that one or more letters have been left out – see 'don't' (i.e. do not) in line 18.
(b) to show possession, when placed before or after an 's' – see 'Bevan's writ' (line 25): 'Britain's post-war housing history' (line 31).

The possessive form is written as follows:
(a) if the possessor is singular, as 's, e.g. the girl's dress, the boy's coat.
(b) if the possessor is singular and the word ends in s, just add an apostrophe, e.g. Frances' dress, Charles' coat.

(c) if the possessor is plural, that is, it ends in 's' already, then add an apostrophe, e.g. the girls' dresses, the boys' coats.
(d) if the possessor is plural and does not end in 's', then add the apostrophe and an 's', e.g. the women's dresses, the children's coats.

Note that pronouns in the possessive do not have an apostrophe by tradition, i.e. yours, hers, ours, theirs.

In the following, change the words in brackets into a shortened form, leaving out letters, or into the possessive form, using the apostrophe. You may have to change the word order.
(a) The one-ness (of the community).
(b) The great roads (of London).
(c) The old people (will not) be asked.
(d) The funerals (of their friends).
(e) Standards (have not) been universally depressed.
(f) The Home (for the Old People) (is not) well run.
(g) We (shall not) buy a house this year.
(h) (Let us) save up for a mortgage.
(i) The council is building a new lavatory (for men).
(j) (It is) not a conservation zone.

Vocabulary

Plurals

Some of the words in the passage form their plurals in an irregular way (not just by adding an 's' – which is the regular way), e.g. communities (line 2–3), authorities (line 7), colonies (line 18), oddities (line 31) and ghettoes (line 35).

(a) Nouns ending in -y preceded by a consonant change the 'y' to 'ies' in the plural, e.g. lady, ladies; family, families. Nouns ending in -y preceded by a vowel form the plural by adding 's', e.g. monkey, monkeys; valley, valleys.
(b) Some nouns ending in -f or -fe change this to -ves in the plural. They are: calves, halves, knives, lives, loaves, selves, (yourselves, etc.), sheaves, shelves, thieves, wives, wolves.

The plural of hoof can be hoofs or hooves; scarf can be scarfs or scarves; wharf can be wharfs or wharves; staff can be staffs or staves (depending on the sense).

All other nouns ending in -f or -fe just add 's', e.g. cliffs, dwarfs, roofs.

(c) Nouns ending in -ch, -s, -sh, -ss, -x form the plural by adding -es, e.g. bench, benches; bus, buses; dash, dashes; pass, passes; fox, foxes.
(d) A number of nouns form the plural by changing the vowel, e.g.
foot, feet; goose, geese; louse, lice.
(e) Nouns ending in -o preceded by a vowel form the plural by adding 's', e.g. cameos, radios, cuckoos. Nouns ending in -o preceded by a consonant tend to form the plural by adding '-es', e.g. cargoes, heroes, potatoes. But there are many exceptions, e.g. photos, pianos, solos.
(f) Most compound nouns form the plural by changing or adding to the most important word, e.g. brothers-in-law, lookers-on. Words like 'bucketful' add 's' to the end, e.g. bucketfuls, spoonfuls.
(g) Some nouns have the same form in the singular and the plural, e.g. sheep, salmon.
(h) Some nouns are almost always used in the plural, e.g. trousers, eaves.

(i) Write down the plurals of the following:
Chief	Negro
Leaf	Dynamo
Gas	Manifesto
Box	Deer
Brush	Aircraft.

(ii) Try to find ten words which have only plural forms, such as 'trouser', and 'eaves', e.g. measles.

Gender

In the passage, 'Housing Minister' (line 30) is used whether the person holding the office is a man or woman. But some words have a different form for the male and female, e.g. dog – bitch; Sir – Madam.

Write down the female form of each of the following:
Actor	Hero
Bachelor	Negro
Boar	Nephew
Fox	Waiter
Heir	Wizard.

Unit 26

Minute writing

The official records of meetings are called the *minutes* and are usually kept in a special book and typed out and given to members before the next meeting. Someone is responsible for making notes during the proceedings and writing them up later as 'minutes', to be heard at, or read before, the next meeting. If approved as a correct record, the minutes are then signed by the Chairman.

The minutes make up a history of the business conducted by the society or club. They are not full reports of every word that is uttered but records of the main items and decisions taken for future reference. Nevertheless, they should not be careless or sketchy. The techniques of report-writing, summarizing and the use of reported speech are all needed in minute writing.

Here is a list of the minimum requirements for minutes:
(a) Heading, with the full name of the society, branch, etc.
(b) Time, date and place of the meeting.
(c) Name of the chairman.
(d) Members present.
(e) Reading of minutes of the previous meeting.
(f) Matters arising from the minutes.
(g) Business conducted at the meeting, taken in order and numbered.
(h) Date of the next meeting.
(i) Time of closing.

Notes
(a) Any *motions* put to the meeting must be recorded exactly and in full. It is, therefore, important to write them down word for word in your notes and not trust to luck for later reconstruction.
(b) The names of proposers and seconders of motions should be recorded, with the number of votes for, against and abstentions.
(c) If a decision is made without a formal motion being put, it is recorded as 'It was resolved'.
(d) Any special ruling by the Chairman on procedure should be recorded.
(e) Officials are usually mentioned by their office rather than by name: 'The Treasurer reported . . .'.

(f) Remember that minutes give an *objective* record of what took place, and not a biased view. An unruly meeting can be reduced to order in the minute book, perhaps more easily than by the Chairman. The phrase 'after discussion' can conveniently condense a great deal of argument.

Good practice can be obtained by getting hold of the word-for-word report of a meeting and putting it into the concise form of minutes. The reports of Parliamentary debates in some of the newspapers can be used in this way.

Write the minutes for the following Council Housing Committee which is hearing reports on repairs to four council properties.

Property 1

The Clerk: Old fittings were to be removed from the outside lavatory of a house dating from around 1900, and a new slimline installation fitted.

The Chairman: Two estimates were received, one from a plumber for £33, the second, for £24, from a firm specialising in house repairs for owner-occupiers. The lower quotation was accepted, although it contained a number of conditions, including one which stated that making good would not be carried out unless specifically asked for. In fact the figure of £24 was exceeded by £7 on account of extra fittings and a lavatory seat.

The Accountant: The verbal estimate was given immediately by telephone and a written estimate arrived six days later. The workmen turned up on the appointed date.

The Surveyor: Original estimate reasonable, but the specific conditions were unusual, and a charge made for extra fittings obtained by the workmen was quite unjustified. The estimate was ambiguous about the supply of a new lavatory seat and this eventually resulted in the householder being charged an extra £4.50, in addition to £2.50 for the extra fittings. Generally the work was well and neatly done. Wall surfaces had not been made good, but this was in the terms of the estimate. On the other hand an overflow pipe was not fitted in the usual way to extend through the outside wall, and although the new fittings had a built-in overflow the effect of this would be to flood the floor – there being a wooden threshold which would effectively dam the water in. No allowance was made in the final bill for an exterior overflow not being provided.

Councillor Smith: There was much to-and-froing after the workmen arrived on account of the wrong fittings having been ordered up, and the cistern they brought was scratched, so they had to go away to get another one. We were surprised when they suggested fitting the old wooden seat to the new loo, and agreed for a pricey bakelite to be got and fitted rather than spoil the job. In discussing the overflow, the plumber told us the inside one would be quite all right. On the whole we felt that it was a reasonably neat job.

Property 2
The Clerk: A brick wall was to be built between two existing outside house walls to make an exterior room. Door and window frames to be built into it.
The Chairman: One estimate was accepted from a freelance bricklayer, who worked with a mate. The price was £20, excluding the cost of bricks, sand and cement, and lintels. An additional £10 was quoted for putting a lintel into a window arch in the house wall and bricking-in above.
The Accountant: Bricklayer and mate turned up when they said they would and did the job quickly.
The Surveyor: Estimate was reasonable for weekend work. Standard of workmanship throughout was good, except that mortar was dropped on wall ties, and joints between window and door frames and brickwork were not sealed. Frames were not pinned to framework, but since the brickwork was still 'green' – i.e. the mortar not hard set – this was allowable, and the workmen took care to leave marks showing where the carpenter should pin subsequently. The new brickwork was broken into adjoining walls every three or four courses, making for strong construction.
Councillor Jones: The men worked through Saturday and a Sunday morning, were quick, neat and pleasant, and the job has proved thoroughly sound. As an extra not charged for, they set hangers into existing walls to take roof joists.

Property 3
The Clerk: Householder wanted old linoleum taken up and new linoleum laid on suitable sub-floor covering, with edging strip to perimeter.
The Chairman: Estimates were received from two contractors, and the slightly lower one of £29.95 was accepted.
The Accountant: Both estimates were given at short notice. The chosen contractors postponed the starting date by a week, and then turned up a day late – unexpectedly, not having sent a message.
The Inspector: Estimates reasonable. The existing sub-floor

was a badly worn surface, and the contractor treated this satisfactorily with latex and hardboard before laying the linoleum and fixing edging strip. Sub-floor covering and linoleum laying were carried out in a competent manner: workmanship and standard of cutting were good.

Councillor Brown: The job has been done very well. However, apart from the delays in starting, they left old linoleum and a roller in the porch for three days, and when they did collect they didn't ring the bell to ask for gluepots and left-over linoleum and some other equipment. I had to telephone them to remind them.

Property 4

The Clerk: In a small basement storeroom under the front entrance steps of a house there was evidence of dampness, spoiling of decorations and plaster. Cement rendering to steps above was badly cracked, letting water in.

The Chairman: Three similar estimates were obtained, the one chosen being £115. Basically the work involved was asphalting the steps to make them completely waterproof. All estimates were given promptly.

The Accountant: Work was promised for the same weekend as the builder carried out his inspection, but no-one turned up to prepare the steps for the asphalter, and when he arrived on the Sunday he was unable to start. Both preparation and asphalting were carried out in the following week.

The Surveyor: Asphalting the steps and re-rendering the inside of the balustrade walls had been well done. I think the coping to the balustrade wall should have been done at the same time, as well as some other rendering, but the householder's opinion was that this could be done later.

Councillor Brown: I thought the job was very well done, except that the top step – York stone which needed patching – was not made completely flat in the recovering process, so that water collects a little. There was also some carelessness in taking away the wooden framing in which the new step was formed; when it was removed a large part of the step was taken with it. I think the asphalter was obviously very good, but the firm's co-ordination with him was poor. It would have been too expensive to have had the copings and other renderings done, and time will tell whether the surveyor was right.

Discussion

Discuss each of the following (for 15 minutes each?). A different third of the group should listen to each discussion and present the minutes later. Remember to appoint a Chairman.
(a) That skilled workers should be paid twice the rate of unskilled ones.
(b) That all building work should be done by a nationally owned firm.
(c) That young people should be called up for compulsory armed or social service at the age of 18.

Unit 27

Multiple Choice Comprehension

Read the passage below, and then answer the questions following it.

Most of the 'specialist' loft converters have tried to develop a standard specification to sell as a package. By using commission salesmen, elaborate sales aids, and national advertising they have gone out and sold the concept all over the country. Their stereotyped conversions have satisfied many.

However, as the distance they operate from their base means that they have to use gangs of sub-contract labour-only workers, the pendulum of success often swings violently the other way, with a client let down rather badly. Also, loft conversions cover an infinite variety of permutations dependent on the requirements of the individual. As houses vary, so do their owners' tastes, ideas, and feelings for them. Very often, one of the reasons why you want to enlarge and not move is because your home has character, so that the last thing you want to do is put up or add on a hurriedly constructed 'box'.

The best way for the discerning house-owner to ensure this project is to find a competent building company which has either an in-house or associated design facility and which will produce a tailor-made job. If the firm is based near you it will have a local reputation to keep up so that you will be less likely to be let down. You might live in an old Edwardian or Victorian terraced house, so make sure that you use stock bricks to blend in with the existing brickwork – using the same bond and mortar colour. If your house is of stone you will now find it impossible to match it, but you can get reconstituted stone blocks that look and feel as if they were hewn out of the same rock with which the house was built.

The whole art of loft conversion is to make it look as if it was always that way. It is important to make it blend internally as well as externally. A new loft conversion should merge with the other rooms in the house and it is worth paying attention to such detail as skirtings, architraves, and door furniture.

Bill Eykyn *Guardian Special Report*

1 'Specialist' (line 1) is most probably inside inverted commas because the loft converters
   A have no real claim to that description
   B all need a long period of training
   C do not remain in business for long
   D all include this word in their advertisements
   E have given no satisfaction to their customers
2 A 'standard specification' (line 2) is best explained as
   A a particular way of selling work
   B an organized process of building
   C an agreed method of constructing
   D an unwritten proposal of contract
   E a fixed description of construction work
3 Which of the following is closest in meaning to 'package' (line 2)?
   A Fair deal
   B Pleasant surprise
   C Manageable idea
   D Complete unit
   E Real bargain
4 Which one of the following words is closest in meaning to 'stereotyped', as used in line 5?
   A Disappointing
   B Dull
   C Fitting
   D Small
   E Unvarying
5 'Specialist' loft converters have sold the idea of a standard loft specification by
   (i) employing salesmen who are paid by results
   (ii) travelling widely
   (iii) using elaborate aids
   (iv) opening shops
   (v) advertising their services throughout the country
       A (i), (ii) and (iii) only
       B (i), (iii) and (v) only
       C (ii), (iii) and (iv) only
       D (ii), (iii) and (v) only
       E (iii), (iv) and (v) only
6 According to the article, the main cause of clients being 'let down badly' (line 9) is that loft converters have to
   A use totally unskilled labour
   B adapt quickly to the demands of the market
   C work far away from their headquarters
   D tackle a wide variety of roof types
   E deal with difficult householders

7 The movement from success to failure (line 8–9) is described in terms of a
  A clock
  B lift
  C pump
  D saw
  E swing

8 According to the passage, one reason why people prefer to enlarge their houses rather than to move is because their house
  A has real possibilities
  B is cheap to run
  C is comfortable to live in
  D is convenient to reach
  E has special features

9 According to the passage the best way to ensure that a loft conversion fits in well with the rest of the house is to
  A own a standard-sized house for a standard unit
  B insist that original building material is used throughout
  C use only local builders and materials for the job
  D find an efficient builder who can offer individual designs
  E have the extension made off-site and set into the house

10 According to the passage, another way in which a householder can ensure that his loft conversion is done satisfactorily is to find a builder
  (i) with a solid financial base
  (ii) in the vicinity of his house
  (iii) as careful as a tailor
  (iv) with a good name to maintain
        A (i) and (ii) only
        B (i) and (iii) only
        C (ii) and (iii) only
        D (ii) and (iv) only
        E (iii) and (iv) only

11 According to the passage, in order to ensure that a loft conversion fits in with a Victorian terraced house, the builder should use
  (i) bricks of stock size
  (ii) designs from Victorian times
  (iii) mortar coloured like the original
  (iv) builders of long standing
        A (i) and (ii) only
        B (i) and (iii) only
        C (ii) and (iii) only
        D (ii) and (iv) only
        E (iii) and (iv) only

12 According to the passage, stone for a loft conversion to a Victorian house that is identical to the original is usually
   A expensive to buy
   B available from demolished houses
   C impossible to obtain
   D obtainable from the original quarry
   E easy to work
13 'Reconstituted', as used in line 27, means that the stone is
   A roughly shaped
   B hand-carved
   C dark-coloured
   D hollow-centred
   E artificially made
14 'The whole art of loft conversion' (line 29) is to ensure that the conversion
   A keeps to the original design and costs
   B has the same skirting boards, architraves and door furniture
   C looks as if it is part of the original building
   D is made of the same materials as the original
   E blends with the houses of the neighbourhood

Summary

Using only the material in the passage above, describe in 100 words what a householder should do to obtain a thoroughly satisfactory loft conversion.

Writing

(a) Describe a loft conversion that you have seen or heard of.
(b) Describe the layout of decoration of a room you would like built for yourself in a loft space.
(c) Describe the advantages and disadvantages of working for a small firm.
(d) Write an advertisement for a firm, specializing in converting empty lofts into rooms, to be placed:
   (i) in a national newspaper;
   (ii) for a short television commercial (remember to describe what the viewer will see).

Oral

(a) A talk should be well planned beforehand and three aspects of it should be kept in mind while preparing and giving the talk.

Firstly, the content should be relevant and organized, and spiced with a little humour for the audience, for whom it should not be too technical or too long.

Secondly, the talk should be easy to hear, clearly spoken and flow without too much hesitation, so that it is a pleasure to hear.

Thirdly, the speaker should communicate with his audience, not only by offering organized and hearable material but by variations in pitch and tone in the voice and by the use of gestures and expressions.

(b) Imagine that you are selling loft conversions in an area. Write down the notes for a talk that you are to make to a group of householders whom you hope to make into customers. Point out:
  (i) why a loft conversion is desirable;
  (ii) the snags that can arise;
  (iii) how a loft should be converted;
  (iv) the effect during loft conversion work on a house;
  (v) the expenses involved.

Do not write out the whole talk, but only sufficient notes, which can easily be read at a distance.

Give part of the talk to your classmates: (discuss, in a friendly way, the speaker's fluency, clarity, liveliness, communication and content).

(c) Write out an imaginary telephone conversation between a foreman on a building site and his employer in an office some distance away about:
  (i) essential materials failing to arrive;
  (ii) workmen threatening to walk off due to piece-rate misunderstandings;
  (iii) a shortage of certain skilled men;
  (iv) an emergency due to an accident;
  (v) rumours that the site is about to be closed down.

Unit 28

Comprehension

Read the following two passages, and then answer the questions following them.

Passage A
It was not until 1933 – some fifteen years after the end of the First World War in 1918 which left a desperate housing shortage – that private money poured lavishly into housebuilding. Before that date, high interest rates and building costs and the attraction of other outlets for capital made investment in housing unprofitable. In short, the building boom of the thirties was largely the product of general slump. Labour was plentiful, wages were low, the cost of building materials had dropped, interest rates were depressed. Only in these conditions did the machine begin to function. Earlier, the attempts to start a housing drive had petered out, and in the early twenties in particular the chief burden was carried by local authorities.

Moreover, even when the high rate of building was attained, the bulk of the new houses were built for the middle classes and for sale and certainly not for those whose housing conditions were most wretched. In the whole period between the two wars, i.e. 1918 to 1939, only one out of every fifteen new houses was to clear slums or relieve over-crowding.

At the end of the Second World War, in 1945, large numbers of building workers and multitudes of those who produced building materials were in the armed forces. The pre-war building force of well over a million men had been sucked into southern England where the ravages of bombing attacks had been most severe; many of them were old and feeble or too young to have learnt their trade. In wartime conditions most building contracts had been placed on a 'cost-plus' basis which was notoriously inefficient.

Britain had had twelve and a half million houses in 1939. Nearly one of every three of these was damaged in the war and those undamaged had mostly gone six years without repairs. Two hundred and eight thousand houses had been totally destroyed, 250,000 were made uninhabitable, 250,000 more had been seriously mauled. In short, by the end of 1945, the population of Britain was squeezed into some 700,000 fewer houses than the country had possessed six years before and no one knew precisely how gross was the unsatisfied pre-war demand even for the barest shelter and comfort. No one knew, further, that in the three post-war years there would be 11 per cent more marriages and 33 per cent more births than in pre-war years. And less still was it realized that full employment and new expectations would increase the numbers of people demanding separate houses far beyond anything which the figures themselves indicated.

Michael Foot *Aneurin Bevan*, Volume 1

Passage B
We all know that the annual rate of building, in the private sector, has dipped, recovered and dropped again over the past ten years. Yet the number of mortgage advances has increased by $12\frac{1}{2}$%. A greater *proportion* of purchasers are relying upon building society money to assist them in their purchase.

The amount of cash advanced, during the same period, has doubled. So a few more people are borrowing a lot more money. As the average cost of a house has vastly increased during the same period this would appear to make sense. But the average cost of a new house went up – not by 100% – but by 140%. Cash advanced up by 100%; purchase price of new houses up by 140%. What does it all mean? More people are buying bigger houses and are having to find more of their own money to do it. It would seem fair to suggest that many of these would, by necessity, be second purchasers, able to use the balance from the sale of their first home.

Ten years ago, nearly 50,000 houses and flats of one and two bedrooms were built in the private sector. Next year it is doubtful whether the figure will reach 30,000. This cannot be a change in the demand pattern; it must be a change in the pattern of supply. Yet how ludicrous it is that, in these years of spiralling inflation and money shortages, we are being forced to produce the luxury item, not as an extension of an otherwise satisfied market, but because the meeting of these more important and basic needs is no longer financially viable.

There is the huge backlog of would-be purchasers: there is the under-developed market of urban renewal (and land reclamation); and the hitherto untapped market, now swollen to bursting point, of the bed-sit dwellers. If the price of land can be pegged (i.e. become cheaper, in real terms), small unit/high density mass-produced dwellings can, even at today's high interest rates, become available to young couples at repayment rates below that at which many are currently paying in rent, and certainly within the 'safe' limit of 25% of income.

What I do know is that we are not going to solve our housing problems by building more and more larger houses, for the better-to-do, especially as many of these will always remain under-occupied. Perhaps the answer lies in high density mass production and to hell with Parker Morris?

from *House Builder*

According to one or both passages:
(a) What were the problems in housing between 1918 and 1939?
(b) What were the problems in housing after 1945?
(c) What have been the problems in housing during the last ten years?
(d) What was done in house building between 1918 and 1939?
(e) What needs to be done in housebuilding in the future?
(f) What part has been played by money in influencing house building since 1918?
(g) Which parts of the housing market have been neglected since 1918?
(h) What are the attitudes of the two writers to their articles? What evidence is there of their attitudes?
(i) What evidence does the author of Passage B offer to illustrate his statement in the third paragraph that there has been 'a change in the pattern of supply'?

Note-making

(a) Referring to the material in the two passages, write the notes for talks to a political group on how you would have dealt with the housing problem, in order to solve it:
   (i) between 1918 and 1939,
   (ii) after 1945,
   (iii) in the last 10 years.
(b) Write the notes for talks to be given to a group of people at a social club on:
   (i) how to dress well without spending too much money;
   (ii) how to be happy as a teenager;
   (iii) how to get on in the building industry;
   (iv) how to make and save money;
   (v) how to make and keep friends.

(c) Write notes to be used by you in the following discussions:
   (i) Should divorce be made harder than at present?
   (ii) Should abortion be made more difficult to obtain?
   (iii) Should parents interfere in their teenage children's lives?
   (iv) Should young people do two years of national service of some kind?

All or parts of the talks of discussion could be held in the students' group.

Unit 29

Oral Work

The document below is the text of a talk on 'Housing People with Special Difficulties', which your boss is to deliver. Having written it out in full, however, he decides to speak from a set of notes, which he asks you to draw up.

He stresses that he wants a set of notes, a plan that will act as a reminder to him, *not* a precis of the talk. 'I need a clearly marked plan, with "prompt headings" for each section and the basic information within each section: *all clearly laid out* so that I can see at a glance where I've got to, and where I'm going.' He adds: 'I've tried to anticipate the sort of questions I'll be asked when I've finished, but if you think of any likely questions, would you add them? You should put the questions in a clearly marked section at the end of the notes.'

Text of Talk

While it would be quite wrong to suggest that there is no longer any need for the majority of Local Authorities to concern themselves with the provision of new housing, there is little doubt that the nature of the housing problem has been changing. Few would deny that the easily identifiable national housing problem with the common characteristics of acute housing shortage in every area, which was for so long an accepted part of our national life, has given way to a whole series of separate problems which vary in type and intensity according to local circumstances.

This change in emphasis has been matched by a growing realisation of the need for local authorities to take a much wider view of their responsibilities, and if a spur was needed this was provided by the Housing Finance Act, 1972. All that was missing was an opportunity for local authorities to rethink their housing policies without the constraints of existing committee structures and chief officer hierarchies. The reorganization of local government provides the answer, and the majority of new housing authorities will surely seize the opportunity to create truly comprehensive housing departments charged with responsibility for all aspects of the housing problem.

But apart from making necessary changes in management and committee structures and departmental organization, it is to be hoped that the new authorities will re-examine existing priorities, expecially in the provision and letting of council housing. They could do worse than look at the special needs of the one-parent family, the large families, students, the homeless and the disabled.

One-parent families obviously have special problems, and not only find it hard to compete for non-council accommodation, but in many cases, as new applicants, find themselves at the bottom of the Council housing list because, until disaster in the shape of bereavement or divorce struck, the need to register an application did not arise.

There are still many who are prepared to argue that any responsibility for the provision of accommodation for students lies with the education authority. The logic of this argument is hard to follow, because however comforting it may be to dismiss it as a housing problem, the hard fact is that students, left to their own devices will, if need be, move into the private rented market, and any backwash will be felt in housing rather than in educational circles.

Those authorities who have carried out surveys as required by the Chronically Sick and Disabled Persons Act have been staggered to find how high is the incidence of physical and mental disability, and how often difficulties are intensified by unsuitable accommodation. Certainly the degree of need is not matched by the degree of special housing provision. How many authorities are currently making sure that even a small proportion of all new dwellings are suitable for occupation by persons of some degree of disability by providing wide door openings and shallow ramped entrances instead of steps; waist-level electric socket outlets; space for a wheelchair against a toilet, and so on? Such features, if incorporated in the original design, can be provided at a fraction of the cost of adaption at a later date, and do not even inhibit the letting of the dwelling to a family without a handicapped member if provision in any area should outstrip demand.

Some local authorities have found that by merely forgetting their normal allocation rules and offering, in collaboration with a local mental hospital, suitable houses to groups of long-term patients, they have given them an opportunity to readjust and resume their place in the general community.

Reorganisation will not in itself solve any problem, but if in the field of housing it does no more than encourage everyone concerned to take a fresh look at housing priorities, then those with special needs at least may have occasion to be thankful.

What is needed is a change of attitude, an acceptance of the fact that local authorities have a special responsibility towards those who are least able to solve their own problems, and a determination to make certain that those with special needs get the special degree of priority to which they are entitled.

Speech-making is an art, one that is useful at weddings and presentations and it is essential in union and political life. Speech-making needs thought and practice. Here are some suggestions on the subject.
(a) Make notes that are short and clear in writing large enough to read at a distance (some speakers use a different colour of ink for different pitches and tones of voice).
(b) Practise speaking before a mirror and with a tape recorder. Ask yourself if your facial and arm gestures are right, or too little, or too exaggerated. Listen to your voice on the tape. Is it varied enough? Is it too slow or too fast; too loud or too soft? Is it clear? Does it stress well?
(c) Make notes for the following speeches and give one of the speeches to your group:
    (i) Saying farewell to a fellow worker;
    (ii) Saying farewell to a fellow union worker;
    (iii) Speaking on behalf of your workmates to your employer asking for:
        more pay; better working conditions;
    (iv) Speaking on behalf of a candidate:
        for union office; at a political meeting;
    (v) At a friend's coming-of-age party;
    (vi) At a friend's wedding.
(d) Make notes for a speech to a political party meeting (of some kind) entitled 'Equal Pay for Equal Work, today'.

Summary

The following passage has been taken from an article dealing with equal pay for men and women. *Using only the information given in the passage*, write a report, consisting of *two* paragraphs, summarizing:

(a) the arguments for giving men and women equal pay for equal work, and
(b) the arguments against giving men and women equal pay for equal work.

Your report should not exceed 150 words altogether. Select the arguments required, arrange them in a sensible order within the appropriate paragraph, *and write in clear and concise English.* Some words or expressions cannot be accurately or economically replaced, but do not copy out long expressions or whole sentences; *use your own words as far as possible. State at the end the number of words you have used.*

Governments in recent years have been in favour of the principle of 'equal pay for equal work'. This support for what is an obvious and undeniable human right has come about because the nation cannot afford to waste a large proportion of its potential labour force by discouraging women from working through unjust treatment in wages and salaries. If girls are rewarded equally with boys they will be similarly encouraged to look upon their jobs as careers and to study for the necessary qualifications. Some argue, however, that if women are lured to go out to work they will neglect their families and there will be an increase in marriage-breakdowns and delinquency in children, who really do need their mothers at home with them.

Our society still imposes more responsibilities on men than on women in financial matters; it is the men who are expected to be the bread-winners, provide the family house, and pay the hundred and one bills which fall through the letter-box. Yet some women have responsibilities equal to those of some men and require just as much money to support and bring up children or to look after aged parents; it is not fair that they should be penalised merely because of their sex. Single women, too, have expenses similar to those of single men – they have to pay for flats, buy clothes, find fares to go to work, and save up for holidays; there is no justification for automatically paying them less than their male counterparts. In any case, some women are better than men in some jobs but nobody suggests that they should receive more; 'unequal' pay never acts to the advantage of women.

Prejudice still maintains that women cannot expect equal pay, because they are suited in some way to the less demanding and repetitive jobs, and because they cannot tolerate the physical and mental strains which accompany the better-paid posts usually occupied by men. Such discrimination against women in what they can earn denies them any dignity in work and adds to their frustration. The exclusion of women from the 'top' jobs by denying them equal pay has resulted in women being in fierce competition with one another, and with some men in the lower posts, so that employers have been able to keep wages low and resist any claims for the improvement of pay scales. In some cases, employing women has meant that some men have lost their jobs because firms have preferred to employ women at lower rates than they would have had to pay to unskilled men. Equal pay for equal work would stop or discourage the continuation of depressed wages and the exploitation of those who work in unskilled jobs.

It is a fact, however, that women are reluctant to accept shift work, which involves periods of night work, and if they are not prepared to accept equal conditions of work with men they can hardly expect equal pay. Women seem to lose more time from work than men owing to sickness or family problems; some regard their jobs only as stop-gaps until they marry and leave. Employers cannot be expected to provide equal opportunities for both boys and girls to learn a trade when experience shows that women often leave a year or two after training in order to marry and set up home; they prefer to devote their training opportunities and financial incentives to young men from whom they can expect about forty years of continuous service. The introduction of equal pay, therefore, may well result in women finding it difficult to secure jobs in competition with men.

Unit 30

Multiple Choice Comprehension

Read the following passage, and then answer the questions on it.

According to my mother, tradesmen had the best jobs in the world. They were independent of any one employer, and, more important, of any one town. Once a lad had served his time he could always try some other job, knowing that failure wouldn't be the end of the world. As far as Mother was concerned, a trade was the finest personal insurance policy in the world. And I can understand why. She hated my Dad working shifts in the glass-works in St Helens. She hated the fact that he was tied down to one employer and one town. Dad was more sceptical about tradesmen, partly because he'd seen some so-called trades eliminated at Pilkington's.

My first job was to brew tea. Then a tall plasterer named Alf Smith, who looked like a local version of Lee Marvin, handed me an empty putty-drum and a spike-headed hammer and told me to make a brazier and get a coke fire going. I took the putty-drum outside and nipped into the next house to examine their brazier. It was perfectly round and with a regular series of holes punched in it, large at the bottom and small at the top. I marched back to my unblemished drum and gave it a sharp belt in the middle with the pointed end of the hammer. Disaster: the whole side of the drum caved in and there was only one microscopic puncture in the metal. I tried to straighten the side back into shape by forcing my foot into the drum. Gradually I prised down the indentation – and my foot shot through the bottom. Immediately the metal sprang back, trapping my leg. I couldn't force it apart with my hands so I clomped across the road and forced the handle of a spade into the drum and withdrew my leg. It was bleeding.

Next I grabbed a spar about six foot long, wedged the drum under the wheel of a concrete mixer and began levering the crumpled side into shape. Then suddenly the opposite side of the drum collapsed and I landed on my back in a puddle. By this time I was fighting mad and hammered blow after blow on the drum. It wilted, warped, and flattened. It was only then I realised that I had an audience: the new gang of plasterers had been watching the performance from the sanctuary of the houses. Some of them were almost speechless with laughter. I was so angry I felt I could burst. Alf Smith came loping out of the house with a new putty-drum. 'That was a technical piece of artistry if ever I saw it,' he said. He took me across to where the sand was stored and carefully filled the drum with sand. Then, with a series of light taps with the hammer, he punched a neat line of holes in the side of the drum, with a fraction of distortion. As I carried the completed brazier back to the house, Alf asked me whether I knew the difference between a wise man and a fool. 'A wise man knows what he doesn't know and a fool doesn't. And you can tell a wise man because he'll ask when he doesn't know and a fool won't. OK?'

'My Apprenticeship' by R. Houlton from *The Listener*

1 The writer's mother believed that tradesmen had the best jobs in the world for all of the following reasons **except** that they
   A were not dependent on anyone
   B had a secure job behind them for ever
   C were assured of rapid promotion
   D would find a job even away from home
   E were free to explore other work

2 The writer's father did not share his wife's faith about learning a trade mainly because he
   A believed newly educated scientists would see that tradesmen were eliminated
   B had realized that outside the glassworks tradesmen had little future
   C considered new industries required either machine-hands or scientists
   D had already seen jobs labelled as 'trades' disappear in one company
   E thought shift work was bound to destroy a man and his job

3 The writer was probably asked to brew the tea for the plasterers because they
   A knew he was good at it
   B thought it would keep him busy
   C had been told it was part of his job
   D gave this work traditionally to juniors
   E wanted him to have an easy time at first

4 The writer 'nipped into the next house to examine their brazier' (lines 16–17) to find out
   A how the holes were arranged
   B if theirs was round like his
   C whether he could borrow theirs
   D if he could get someone to help
   E how he should hold the hammer
5 'Microscopic' (line 22) suggests that the hole he had made was
   A uneven in shape
   B impossible to find
   C out of position
   D difficult to mend
   E hard to see
6 Which of the following means most nearly the same as 'prised' as it is used in line 24?
   A Forced
   B Stamped
   C Levered
   D Kicked
   E Squeezed
7 'Clomped' (line 27) suggests that his walk across the road was
   A dangerous
   B clumsy
   C secretive
   D painful
   E hurried
8 The author was 'fighting mad' (line 34) most probably because he
   A was frustrated at not being able to do the job
   B thought the plasterers were laughing at him
   C had hurt his leg which was bleeding
   D realized the men had played a joke on him
   E believed that the time allowed had almost run out
9 'Wilted, warped, and flattened' (line 35) suggests that the final appearance of the drum was all of the following **except**
   A twisted
   B jagged
   C bent
   D dented
   E squashed

10 'Performance' (line 37) suggests that his attempts had been
   A planned beforehand by the author
   B enjoyed by interested spectators
   C dramatized like an actor's on a stage
   D met with loud applause from the audience
   E exaggerated in their violence
11 As Alf Smith appeared with the new putty-drum (lines 39–40) he
   A was still speechless with laughter
   B showed indifference to the boy's troubles
   C took long, careless strides
   D strolled lazily out from nowhere
   E staggered under the drum's weight
12 When Alf Smith said, 'That was a technical piece of artistry if ever I saw it' (lines 40–1) he was being
   A clever
   B truthful
   C disagreeable
   D complimentary
   E sarcastic
13 Alf Smith's distinction between a wise man and a fool (line 47) depends on the fact that a wise man
   (i) needs everything explained to him
   (ii) recognizes his own ignorance
   (iii) distinguishes fools from clever men
   (iv) asks others who know more for help
      A (i) and (ii) only
      B (i) and (iii) only
      C (ii) and (iii) only
      D (ii) and (iv) only
      E (iii) and (iv) only

Notes and research

(a) Write out four questions to ask a Careers Officer who wishes to help you.
(b) Write down four questions to ask a guest speaker who is coming to your College to talk about 'The Construction Industry in the next 20 years'.
(c) Find out the most popular employment for: (i) boys (ii) girls, in your College or area. Does this compare with the national trend?

(d) Write down the answers to the following questions:
    (i) What kind of career do you foresee for yourself?
    (ii) What qualifications do you possess?
    (iii) What qualifications do you need to obtain yet?
    (iv) What are your main interests?
    (v) Have you any special talents and abilities?
(e) Complete the following form to give to a Careers Officer or a Job Centre:
    (i) Name, surname and other names;
    (ii) Address;
    (iii) Age and date of birth;
    (iv) Schools and colleges attended;
    (v) Qualifications obtained;
    (vi) Hobbies and pastimes followed;
    (vii) Clubs and societies joined;
    (viii) Jobs desired, in order of preference;
    (ix) Any other information, i.e. do you prefer working with your mind only or doing more physical work? Do you like working indoors or outdoors?
(f) Build up a file on the career you would like to follow. (It should include pamphlets, advertisements for such jobs, information about working conditions, scope for future promotion, wages, trades union involvement and so forth.)

Notes and report

Find out about the work done by one of your friends or relatives, or see if you can visit a local firm (perhaps through your College) and:
(a) Make notes on the following:
    (i) wages (or salary) at the ages of 16, 20 and 30;
    (ii) hours of work;
    (iii) conditions under which people work;
    (iv) opportunities for further education (day release, etc.);
    (v) opportunities for training;
    (vi) opportunities for promotion;
    (vii) facilities for eating, relaxation, social life.
(b) Write a report based on your notes.

Writing

(a) Write a description of your first day in a new job, telling how it appeared at the time and how it seems in the light of greater experience since.

(b) What are the responsibilities of a young person in accepting a job?
(c) Practical jokes and jokers – describe some you know of.
(d) Write a sketch of your friend at work and of your foreman.
(e) Write the instructions to be attached to the following, remembering that they should be clear, simple and not too long: a spade, a trowel, a hod, a bag of cement, scaffolding.
(f) Write an advertisement for a shop window offering a set of building tools for sale.
(g) Draft an advertisement for a newspaper offering yourself for employment and describing your age, sex, qualifications, personal qualities. (Remember the expense involved.)
(h) Send a telegram to the firm you hope to work for, explaining why you cannot that afternoon attend an interview for a job, due to sickness or train cancellation or family problems, etc. (Remember the expense!)

Unit 31

Suggested Projects

1. An enquiry into local council housing standards, especially sound-proofing and amenities.
2. The materials and building methods used in a local famous (well known) old house.
3. The kinds of provision made in houses for the old and disabled.
4. Check on three or four building or repair jobs to houses done locally and find out about customer satisfaction and disappointment.
5. Do an imaginary repair job to your own house or college and estimate the kinds and costs of material, labour and profits.
6. Investigate the history of a local castle or military building, finding out its materials, methods and costs originally.
7. Find out what schemes of entry and help on entry are given to local building apprentices.
8. See if your local council are engaged in any restoration work and report on the materials, methods and appearance of the restored work.
9. Design a site hut of your own, describing its layout and amenities.
10. Find out what kinds of house conversions are done by firms in your area. Follow one of these conversions through, with the firm's permission, from the original drawings to completion.
11. Find some pre-fabricated building in your area and describe its merits and disadvantages.
12. Describe the housing in your area, paying particular attention to how it suits the people occupying it.
13. Describe a local church or chapel. Describe its original materials, methods of building and costs.
14. Look at some walls in your area. Describe their different materials and textures and functions.
15. Describe your local council's attitude to housing and its provision of council housing: (i) now, (ii) in the future.
16. Describe the history of a local building firm.
17. Describe and compare local houses that were built 100 years ago with those built recently.
18. Describe some of the buildings in your area which are scheduled, as of historic or architectural importance.

Acknowledgments

For permission to use copyright material in this book, the authors and publishers wish to thank the following:

Eyre and Spottiswoode Ltd for an extract from *The Day of the Sardine* by Sid Chaplin; Times Newspapers Ltd for the following extracts: by Colin Chapman *The Sunday Times*, London, September 1965, and from 'How Modern Architects Have Failed Us' by Conrad Jameson adapted from *The Sunday Times*, 6 February 1977; The Daily Telegraph Ltd for an extract by Paul Johnson from the *Telegraph Sunday Magazine*, July 1976; *The Socialist Worker* for an extract from that paper published on 19 August 1972; United Trades Press Ltd for an extract from *Safety on the Site* by B. A. C. White; Pluto Press Ltd for an extract from *The Hazards of Work* by Patrick Kinnersly; Her Majesty's Stationery Office for the use of specified data from the *Report of Her Majesty's Inspector of Factories 1974, CMND 6322*; Routledge and Kegan Paul Ltd for an extract from *Bricks to Build a House* by John Woodforde; Penguin Books Ltd for an extract from *Building Materials* (Industrial Archeology Series, Longman Books, 1972) pp. 72–3 by Kenneth Hudson, and for figures 13, 14 and 15 from *The Buildings of England* series by Nikolaus Pevsner (from the glossary reproduced in each volume); Hutchinson Publishing Group Ltd for an extract from *Carpentry and Joinery* by R. Bayliss; Guardian Newspapers Ltd for extracts from *The Guardian* by Philip Jordan (1 April 1975), by Lynn Owen (1977), by Bill Eykyn for an article entitled 'Best to Call in the Professionals' from a *Guardian Special Report* (November 1976), and for the extract on page 55; B. T. Batsford Ltd for an extract from *How to Look at Old Buildings* by E. Vale; Northwood Publications Ltd for an extract from *The Illustrated Carpenter and Builder*; The Architectural Press Ltd for extracts from *Towards a New Architecture* by Le Corbusier (translated by Etchells), and from *The Modern House* by F. R. S. Yorke; Hodder and Stoughton Ltd for an extract from *Teach Yourself Home Heating* by B. J. King and J. E. Beer; Argus Books Ltd for an extract and artwork from *All About Home Heating* by R. Warring; Robert Graves for a poem in *The Collected Poems of Robert Graves* published by Cassell Ltd; Faber and Faber Ltd for extracts from *The State of Britain* by Sir Colin Buchanan, and from *The Spire* by William Golding; Joan Littlewood Productions Ltd for the advertisement for the 'First Giant Space Mobile'; University of London Schools Examination Department for extracts from the English GCE O Level papers, Summer 1970 and January 1976; Robert Hale Ltd for an extract from *Sir Christopher Wren* by Bryan Little; TUC Education Service for extracts from courses; Northwood Publications Ltd for an extract from the *Building Trades Journal*, September 1976; The Institute of Building for an extract from *Building Technology and Management* by Dr A. J. Wilson, and for another extract from the same magazine (April 1976); K. R. Fines for extracts and artwork from Brighton Planning Department's publication *Extending Your Home*; Business Education Council for an extract from the OND Public Administration Examination in English, June 1975; Davis-Poynter Ltd for an extract from *Aneurin Bevan*, Volume 2 by Michael Foot; Granada Publishing Ltd for an extract from *Aneurin Bevan*, Volume 1 by Michael Foot; Federated Employers Press Ltd for an extract from *House Builder*, May 1974; R. Houlton for an extract from 'My Apprenticeship' in *The Listener*, October 1971.

Every effort has been made to trace and acknowledge ownership of copyright. The publishers will be glad to make suitable arrangements with any copyright holders whom it has not been possible to contact.